Freeing
the
natural
voice

Freeing the natural voice

Kristin Linklater

Drawings by Douglas Florian

Drama Publishers
an imprint of
Quite Specific Media Group Ltd.
New York and Hollywood

This book is dedicated to the memory of
IRIS WARREN
and to those who have trained with me to continue her work
particularly
Rowena Balos, Fran Bennett, Robert Chapline, Bobby Troka
and the Working Theater group.

© 1976 by Kristin Linklater
© 1976 Drawings by Douglas Florian

For information address:
Drama Publishers
an imprint of
Quite Specific Media Group Ltd.
7373 Pyramid Place
Hollywood, CA 90046
email: info@quitespecificmedia.com

Business Office
(212) 725-5377 v.   (212) 725-8506 f.
email: info@quitespecificmedia.com

Quite Specific Media Group Ltd. imprints:
Costume & Fashion Press
Drama Publishers
By Design Press
Jade Rabbit
EntertainmentPro

web: www.quitespecificmedia.com

Library of Congress Cataloging in Publication Data
Linklater, Kristin
        Freeing the natural voice
            1. Voice culture   1. Title
PN4162.L55   808.5   75-28172
ISBN 0-89676-071-5

Printed in Canada

My grateful acknowledgments go to the Ford Foundation for making it feasible for me to take a year away from teaching in order to write this book; to the Rockefeller Foundation for five weeks at the Villa Serbelloni where the atmosphere made writing possible; to Ted Hoffman, Aileen Friedman, Linda Readerman, Andro Linklater and Jean-Claude van Itallie for invaluable editorial assistance; to Arthur Strimling and Gordon Schaye for early reading and feedback and to Tom Shipp for the generosity with which he made his scientific contribution.

Iris Warren: A Memoir

In her introductory chapter, Kristin Linklater explains how her own work and the ideas and method she is describing, were originated by Iris Warren. My job is to try and fill in a little of the background, by saying some more about this very remarkable lady.

I heard of her first from a young actor, and later from a young actress, who were in plays I was directing in London. In both of them I had found a capacity for which I was always looking and too seldom finding: the ability to speak with deep emotion, simply and from the heart. They both assured me that this they had found from working with Iris Warren and that she and I "spoke the same language." It was clear that we must meet.

When we did, we found an immediate identity of interests, professional, philosophic and personal. One of our first long talks was in the garden of a beautiful old farmhouse, about 30 miles from London, but standing alone in a deserted little valley. Iris and her friends had restored the house and created a lovely garden. Iris was an enthusiastic and skillful gardener: a hobby which can be a great help to anyone who teaches. Waiting there while Iris went in to make tea, we noticed lying on the grass a copy of the book, *Zen in the Art of Archery*, which many theatre people have found such a help. I knew then that Iris and I were destined to work happily together.

We soon had the chance. I was asked to take over the London Academy of Music and Dramatic Art. I told Iris that I would only accept it if she would join us; for, while we were both seeking the same thing in acting, she had found a direct technical way to the place in an actor from which it came, and I had only rather blundering, psychological methods and my long theatre experience to guide me.

It was generous of her to accept, for she was then beginning to be at the height of her fame and her studio, where she taught privately, was beseiged by many of the best and most successful young actors and actresses in London, such as Geraldine McEwan, Anna Massey, Joan Greenwood, Harry Andrews; and some of the older generation too: Evelyn Laye, for instance, was one of her most ardent admirers.

She worked amazingly hard, going to a play to see a student at night, then getting up very early to give someone a lesson before their morning rehearsal, but she had great vitality and never seemed tired. She fed, I think, on the happiness of helping people and the joy they found working with her. She was a big woman, what is called Junoesque, and although she could be intimidating, her habitual expression was gentle and serene.

I think one of the things that made working with her such a delight was that she herself was continuously discovering more. Every lesson was for her a new and exciting experience. On the two days a week that she came to us, she would come to my room for a drink when work was over, to tell me the events of the day. Often she would say: "I did something today I've never done before," or "I found something quite new today."

Although she preferred individual to class work, her handling of a class was wonderful. While most completely disciplined, the atmosphere was easy, light and full of warmth and people felt united to her and to each other. It was, at the same time, deeply caring and yet impersonal and professional. I believe this was a large part of the magic she could work. While she had a great understanding of people and could diagnose — it seemed instinctively — the strengths and weaknesses of their temperament and how their best capacities could be realized, no one was ever made to feel that she was intruding on their privacy or that they were being "got at." She worked with the sureness and detachment that one meets in the finest doctors and surgeons. She would calculate most carefully how far a class, or an individual, could go, at what stage in their development and, while always challenging them to go forward, never forced anything.

I think I learned a lot about her quality by seeing her make a mistake. She was guiding an exceedingly tense girl through an exercise designed to produce a very complete release; it was difficult, but she finally succeeded. When the girl went back to her seat she burst into uncontrollable sobs. I was sitting next to Iris and she said quietly but coolly: "Damn! I did that too soon." The next minute the girl was folded to Iris' motherly bosom and all was soon well.

Perhaps this medical detachment was no accident. Iris said that much in her work had grown out of a long and deep friendship with a doctor who was a highly skilled psychologist. She had brought all she had learned from him about the functioning of a human being to bear on the use of the human voice, so that it could do far more than produce a nice sound.

Now it seems necessary to say something about Kristin and how she has come to write this remarkable book. She was a student with us in our early days. We all felt she showed great potential talent as an actress, she had a naturally good voice and took to Iris' work like a duck to water. Iris' time was becoming a great problem as her fame increased. She steadfastly refused to allow anyone else to work on the students' voices, or to train an assistant or successor. Iris was particularly fond of Kristin and I felt would possibly accept her as an assistant. I felt in my bones that this could be very important; both for Iris' work and for Kristin; as indeed it has turned out to be, but only owing to Kristin's talent, determination and intelligence. Iris gave her practically no help. She said: "I don't want her to be a carbon copy of me. She must find it out for herself, as I've done." And that Kristin has certainly done, adding to the work from her own experience, systematizing it and producing this book.

At the time I think Iris was right: and now Kristin is right to have trained others and to have written this book.

It only remains to say that Iris Warren died of cancer in 1963. She worked in great pain almost up to her death. For nearly three years before that only her closest friends knew that she was doomed. Long before this Kristin had ceased to be an assistant and become a fine teacher in her own right.

Michael MacOwan
former Director of the
London Academy of
Music and Dramatic Art

Contents

An introduction to the approach   1

1: *How the voice works*   6

2: *Why the voice does not work*   11

Part one: **The freeing process**

3: *The spine: the support of breath*   19

4: *Breathing: the source of sound*   25

5: *The touch of sound*   35

6: *Vibrations that amplify the initial sound*   41

[Intermission: Workout for relaxation, the spine, the
    head, breathing, touch of sound, humming]   52

7: *The channel for sound*   57

Part two: **The developing process:
the resonating ladder**

8: *The channel resonators*   85

9: *Releasing the voice from the body*   91

[Intermission: Working plan for material in chapters 3
   through 9]   94

10: *The middle of the voice*   97

11: *The nasal resonator*   104

12: *Range*   112

13: *The skull resonators*   115

Part three: **Sensitivity and power**

14: *Breathing power*   121

15: *The center*   135

16: *Articulation*   144

[Intermission: Workout]   164

Part four: **The link to text and acting**

17: *Words*   171

18: *Texts*   184

19: *Observations and opinions on voice
   and acting*   192

An introduction
to the approach

I hope this book will be useful for professional actors, student actors, teachers of acting, teachers of voice and speech and the interested lay person. Its aims are to present a lucid view of the voice in the general context of human communication and to provide a series of exercises to free, develop and strengthen the voice – first as a human instrument, then as the human *actor's* instrument.

The approach is designed to liberate the natural voice rather than to develop a vocal technique. The basic assumption of the work is that everyone possesses a voice capable of expressing, through a two-to-four octave natural pitch range, whatever gamut of emotion, complexity of mood and subtlety of thought he or she experiences. The second assumption is that the tensions acquired through living in this world, as well as defenses, inhibitions and negative reactions to environmental influences, often diminish the efficiency of the natural voice to the point of distorted communication. Hence, the emphasis here is on the removal of the blocks that inhibit the human instrument as distinct from the development of a skillful musical instrument. I must underline at the outset that in our perception of our own voices there is a vital difference to be observed between what is "natural" and what is "familiar."

The objective is a voice in direct contact with emotional impulse, shaped by the intellect but not inhibited by it. Such a voice is a built-in attribute of the body with an innate potential for a wide pitch range, intricate harmonics and kaleidoscopic textural qualities,

which can be articulated into clear speech in response to clear thinking and the desire to communicate. The natural voice is transparent — revealing, not describing, inner impulses of emotion and
thought, directly and spontaneously. The person is heard, not the
person's voice.

To free the voice is to free the person, and each person is indivis-
ibly mind and body. Since the sound of the voice is generated by
physical processes, the inner muscles of the body must be free to
receive the sensitive impulses from the brain that create speech. The
natural voice is most perceptibly blocked and distorted by physical
tension, but it also suffers from emotional blocks, intellectual blocks,
aural blocks, spiritual blocks. All such obstacles are psycho-physical
in nature, and once they are removed the voice is able to communicate the full range of human emotion and all the nuances of thought.
Its limits lie only in the possible limits of talent, imagination or life
experience.

Physical awareness and relaxation are the first steps in the work to
be done, with a constant emphasis on mind-body unity. Breath and
sound must always be connected to thought and feeling so that the
two processes work simultaneously to activate and release inner impulses and to dissolve physical blocks.

This book contains a detailed series of exercises, combining imagery and imagination with technical knowledge, that can lead to
enough understanding of the psycho-physiology of the voice to recondition your habitual way of communicating. The framework of
exercises is impeccably designed and has an enduring potency. Its
architecture is the work of the late Iris Warren.

The particular approach to voice training for actors found in this
book has evolved slowly. It has grown with an era that has revealed
more and more about human functioning. The work began with the
pioneering studies of Elsie Fogerty during the first quarter of this
century in London. She systematized a method of speech training
that was based on the accurate physical mechanics of the voice. During the same period, F. Matthias Alexander was making his invaluable contribution to the understanding of human body behavior.
He showed that habitual patterns of physical usage impose a dicta-
torship on the body which can only be broken with careful psycho-
physical re-conditioning on the deepest level. His influence is clear
in much of the voice work that has developed since then.

It was Iris Warren who moved the science of voice production for
British actors into a new phase by adding psychological understanding to physiological knowledge. In the late thirties Iris Warren began
tackling the most common problem among actors, that of straining
the voice when expressing strong emotions, not by dealing directly
with the suffering voice but by unblocking the emotions. The voice

exercises remained, but were gradually altered by the shift from external, physical controls to internal, psychological ones. The criterion for assessing progress lay in the answer to the question "how does it feel?" rather than "how does it sound?" The ultimate aim was, and is, to free yourself through your voice. Iris Warren's constant emphasis was "I want to hear you, not your voice." This was happening at a time when the "voice beautiful" was still very much in vogue, when pear-shaped vowels and technical skill were preferred to "vulgar" emotion.

The search for an equilibrium between technique and emotional freedom has occupied actor-training for half a century, and in the history of actor development, America and Britain have been consistently out of step with one another. In the thirties, forties and fifties, Stanislavsky's books, the Group Theatre and the Actor's Studio moved American actors forward in psychological and emotional exploration to the point where they virtually abandoned the study of "external skills." In Britain those skills reigned supreme. By the fifties the influence of an emotionally vital American theatre had begun to inspire the British to fill out their technique with more gut content. By the sixties, America, mushrooming with regional repertory companies, was crying out for technique to cope with the range of cultural events from classical to avant-garde.

When, in America, actors tried to find teachers to help them meet this demand, they often found that the technical skills were still being taught as they had been in the twenties through elocution, ballet, singing, gymnastics and phonetics.

Meanwhile, in London, working from outside inwards, ways of developing the actor's being into a sensitive, integrated, creative instrument had grown — originated by Jacques Copeau, developed by Michel St. Denis and Litz Pisk and nurtured at the Old Vic Theatre School. The spirit of this legendary school was carried into the London Academy of Music and Dramatic Art when Michael MacOwan took it over in 1951, beginning a collaboration in actor-training with Iris Warren.

My own work with Iris Warren began when I was an acting student at LAMDA. After completing the program, I spent two years acting in a repertory company, and then was invited back to LAMDA as a student-teacher of voice under Miss Warren. I worked with her, learning and teaching, for six years. In 1963 I decided to come to America to set up my own voice studio.

The voice work that I brought with me had evolved over the years to the point where it married well with the American methods of acting. On the one hand, British theatre was still suffering from a lack of emotional and psychological demands, while, on the other hand, the American theatre was lacking an adequate means of physical and vocal communication; this resulted in an imbalance between the creative use of inner self and communicative skill in both countries.

The balance in my own work was improved by my involvement as vocal coach with various American acting companies, such as the Tyrone Guthrie Theatre, the Lincoln Center Repertory Company (under Robert Whitehead and Elia Kazan) and the Open Theater under Joseph Chaikin. Another strong influence on my development was the acting teacher Peter Kass, with whom I worked in the New York University Theatre Program.

Also it was in America that I was introduced to the Alexander technique, which helped clarify the psycho-physical nature of the voice work.

There is growing psycho-therapeutic and general interest in the interdependence of the mind and body today, and more and more people are discovering that to unlock the mind, it is necessary to unlock the body. The Alexander technique, Rolfing, T'ai Chi and Yoga are all popular physical disciplines that help to free the emotional and psychological self by ridding the body of habitual tensions.

Actors who feel the need for total communication are finding these and similar ways to develop bodies that are sensitive and integrated, rather than super-controlled and muscular; they are also looking for ways to incorporate the voice into this union of self and body. In the psycho-therapeutic context the voice has been neglected, and apart from screaming primally and talking endlessly, little has been done to free it from its prison of environmental influence, unconscious psycho-physical conditioning and aesthetic standardization.

Perfect communication for the actor implies a balanced quartet of intellect and emotion, body and voice—a quartet in which no one instrument compensates with its strength for the weakness of another.

In the following chapters I have tried to capture the work that Iris Warren said should never be written down. It is intended, by its nature, to be conveyed orally, and it is dangerous to limit and define it in printed words. The writing of this book has therefore been resisted for years, but it is now offered in response to demand. In many ways the strength of this approach is the one-to-one relationship between teacher and pupil. No two people, no less two voices, are the same, and each person's problems differ. How do you *teach* relaxation? By touching the pupil's body and feeling whether the muscles are responding to the messages being sent to them. How do you induce a new use of the voice? By taking hold of the body and moving it in new directions which break conditioned, habitual movements. How can the student know that a new experience is a constructive one without feedback from some external and trustworthy guide? To this last question I have no good answer, and do believe that a book is a poor substitute for a class.

It is also important to keep in mind that this book will be difficult to use because it requires dealing with cause rather than effect. It is impossible to use the book superficially because the exercises are concerned more with re-thinking usage than with re-doing sounds.

Whenever possible, I suggest that the serious student work with at least one other person, taking turns reading the instructions and checking the results. Mutual teaching can be very rewarding and it incorporates the central point of voice work, namely communication.

If you have to work alone, you must sacrifice your desire for results to the experience of causes. Although intelligence is needed to understand the exercises, you must abandon intellect when doing them in favor of feelings and sensory impressions. You must not jump to conclusions as to what is right or wrong, because you are already a well-developed censor of self. Nor can you trust your judgment, since it is biased by habitual ideas of good and bad and wary of new experiences.

You will be re-conditioning a way of communicating that has served you, for better or worse, all your life, so that to effect real change you must plan a daily session of at least an hour, over the period of at least a year. Also, realize that you are using your voice throughout the day, and that your exercises can be practiced continually. Even if you do work regularly, progress is slow; in the beginning there will be marked improvement, but this will level off for a time. Most important of all, you must have patience; even after you understand and practice the approach, it may take time before you can experience it in performance. But when you do, the results will be enormously satisfying.

1: How the voice works

Here is a simple physiological outline of the mechanics of the voice:

(1) There is an impulse in the motor cortex of the brain.

(2) The impulse stimulates breath to enter and leave the body.

(3) The breath makes contact with the vocal folds creating oscilla-tions.

(4) The oscillations create vibrations in the breath stream.

(5) The vibrations are amplified by resonators.

(6) The resultant sound is articulated by the lips and tongue to form words.

This picture is easily grasped. It is, unfortunately, a gross over-simplification of an infinitely intricate human process.

Here now is a scientific description:

a. A series of impulses are generated in the motor cortex of the brain and sent through neural pathways to the speech structures.

b. The impulses are timed to arrive at the different locations in the body so that a smooth, coordinated set of actions takes place.

c. First the vocal tract from the lips and nose to the lungs is opened up and the inspiratory muscles of respiration contract to lower pres-sure in the thorax so that air can rush into the lungs relatively un-impeded.

d. When sufficient air has been inspired for the desired utterance, the respiratory system reverses itself and by a combination of elastic recoil of distended tissue and by abdominal and thoracic muscle contraction, forces are developed to push air back up the vocal tract and out the mouth and nose.

e. The larynx, however, has at least partially closed the vocal folds at the beginning of exhalation so that the air stream is now impeded in its upward path.

f. The pliable vocal folds are set into quasi-synchronous vibration as the air passes between them.

g. These vibrations break up the outgoing breath stream into puffs of air that are released into the vocal tract above.

h. These puffs of air excite the air in the resonating cavities of the pharyngeal, oral and nasal passages and produce sound in the upper vocal tracts.

i. The shape, volume and opening of the resonators determines the overtone structure of the sound, while the basic pitch is determined by the rate at which the vocal folds vibrate.

j. Resonation can be thought of as two types: The first type is used to shape or color the voice generated at the larynx regardless of the speech sound intended. The second type is that which modifies the larynx-generated sound for a specific speech sound. The first type of sound is always present for the speaker and the second type depends on what the speaker wants to say — the movements involved in this comprise what is called articulation.

I want to make it clear that from this point on I shall not be using exact scientific terminology. I have chosen to describe the voice metaphorically, analogically and by its perceivable features. While this simplification may make the voice scientist quail it has proven the best approach for the voice user.

Here now is my attempt to describe the complex *psycho*-physical process through which a free voice can work as a human instrument. Take (1) to be the need to communicate (without which the voice has no life). This need becomes an electrical impulse which travels via the spinal cord to the nerve endings that govern the muscles operating the organs of speech. According to the stimulus, this impulse will contain a greater or lesser voltage. Someone says "good morning" to you. If it is someone you see daily and have no particular regard for, the stimulus will be minimal, there will be a small impulse to answer and a slight reaction in the breath and larynx muscles creating just enough vibrations to serve the need of a dutiful response. If it is someone whom you love dearly, whom you are delighted and surprised to see, the stimulus may arouse you emotionally; your solar plexus nerve endings glow with warmth, your breath reacts with vitality and plays vigorously on your vocal folds to make the vibrations dance out through the resonators, serving your need to communicate how you feel. There are infinite variations of external stimuli and internal reactions, and it is impulse, arousing the reflex musculature of speech, that controls their expression.

After the impulse comes the breath response (2). This means that countless muscles throughout the length and breadth of the torso perform an extraordinary set of coordinated movements that expand the rib cage, contract the diaphragm, move the stomach down, shift the intestines around to make room for the expanding lungs, allowing the air cells to suck in air and then, reversing the action, to expel it.

Next in my physiological picture comes (3): the play of breath on the vocal folds. In fact, the respiratory and laryngeal actions are simultaneous, the same impulse that stimulates the breathing musculature activates the laryngeal musculature to stretch the vocal folds so that they offer enough resistance to the breath to oscillate on impact. A gentle pressure of breath meeting relatively relaxed folds creates slower oscillations and the resultant vibrations of sound are of a low frequency. A strong pressure of air finds greater resistance from folds\pulled tighter, and a higher frequency results in a higher pitch. (The folds themselves are not muscles, but membranes, and are not brought into play by the breath; they are lengthened and shortened by the surrounding cartilages to which they are attached, whose muscles react directly to motor impulses from the brain. They are between thirty and fifty millimeters in length.)

The initial vibrations of sound are no more recognizable as such than the vibrations created on piano strings if the hammer were to strike them without a sounding board behind them. But as soon as the breath oscillates the folds, the vibrations that occur re-sound off the nearest sounding boards which are the cartilages of the larynx.

In step (5) of the human musical instrument, "the vibrations are amplified by resonators." Opinions still conflict on how the resonating system works and what approach to take; indeed, it may be adequately described only in terms of advanced physics. For working purposes I use the following practical, tangible description.

The nature of vibrations is to multiply as they meet appropriately resistant textures. They sound again as they bounce off different surfaces, with different quality and quantity determined by the texture of the surface and the shape of the cavity. The re-sounding or resonating surfaces within the body, available to the initial vibrations of sound, are virtually uncountable considering that bone, cartilage, membrane and muscle can all serve as amplifiers and conductors. The harder the surface, the stronger the resonance: bone is best, cartilage is very good, and toned-up muscle can provide a good resonating surface, but a flabby, fleshy, unresistant area will only muffle and absorb vibrations (like heavy velvet or a sponge). The voice finds its most satisfying resonators where there are clearly defined hollows and empty tunnels in the architecture of the body, such as the pharynx, the mouth, the nose; but the bony structure of the chest, the cheekbones, the jawbone, the acoustically powerful sinus hollows, the skull, the cartilages of the larynx and the vertebrae of the spine all contribute resonance.

The inter-relationship of pitch and resonators has to do with suitable apertures, appropriate shapes, large or small cavities; these are all subject to change due to different degrees of tension in the muscle tissue lining that tunes a resonating area to a given pitch.

For working purposes, the pattern of resonating response to changing pitch can be observed as follows: the low sounds get resonance from the chest and lower throat (pharynx); the lower-middle part of the range is amplified from the back wall of the throat through the soft palate, the teeth, the jawbone and the hard palate; moving upwards through the middle voice, resonance comes in from the mid-sinuses, the cheekbones, the nose; finally, the upper-middle and high voice resonate in the upper sinuses above the nose, and in the skull. All the pitches and resonances spill into each other's precincts, creating harmonics and overtones.

In order to demonstrate how this sophisticated musical instrument becomes human in its response to (1), the impulse to communicate, I would like to posit an ideal of how the natural voice would function to communicate the thoughts and a continuum of feelings of a hypothetical human being who is uninhibited, open, sensitive, emotionally mature, intelligent and uncensored.

When he/she is feeling relaxed, warm, comfortable and contented, the muscles are loose, the breathing undisturbed, the energies flowing easily. If there is an impulse to transmit this state through words, it generates just enough extra energy to send breath gently onto the vocal folds which, remaining relatively relaxed, produce a low sound which is resonated through the chest and lower pharynx. A change in mood from lazy contentment to positive happiness or surprise, or impatience, will increase the causal energy which will dispatch the breath with greater vigor onto tighter folds, producing a higher pitch which will ring into the middle resonators of the face. The muscle tissue lining the corridors and caverns of the throat, mouth and mask respond simultaneously to the mood change, and their stretch helps tune the resonators to the pitch generated by the increased energy. If excitement grows, the breath is still more stimulated, the folds tighten more which produces higher sounds; correspondingly, muscles in the upper pharynx stretch and tone up, the soft palate lifts higher and the sound is released into the upper sinuses. Finally, if excitement reaches a pitch commonly regarded as hysterical (perhaps because most people are unaccustomed to operating at that level), the pressure on the folds and their responsive tension will send a scream into the head, which is a superb acoustic dome with a bony resilience capable of dealing with the pressure of such a sound.

This pattern of emotional energy and resonating response is, as I have said, hypothetical, and too simple to encompass defense mechanisms, neuroses, habitually aggressive or habitually passive behavior, but it can provide landmarks in the foggy geography of how we communicate what we feel.

In the final stage of vocal communication the stream of vibrations, flowing unimpeded through richly resonating chambers and out through the mouth, is formed into words. There are eight general areas of articulation in the mouth: two lips, the front of the tongue, the upper gum ridge, the middle of the tongue, the roof of the mouth, the back of the tongue and the back of the hard palate. Consonants are formed when two articulating surfaces meet and interrupt the flow of breath or sound. Vowels are formed as the lips and tongue move to mold the flow of vibrations into different shapes. In the economy with which words are formed lies the accuracy with which they realize thought. The muscles of the body can never respond finely enough to reflect the agility of thought, but the articulating muscles should crave that ability in the interest of accurate revelation of the mind.

2: Why the voice does not work

The voice is prevented from responding with the spontaneity described in the last chapter because that spontaneity depends on reflex action and most people have lost the ability, and perhaps the desire, to behave reflexively. Except in moments "beyond control," such as extreme pain, extreme fear, extreme ecstasy, nearly all visibly reflex behavior is short-circuited by secondary impulses.

These, in general, are protective, and at best give time to think. When, however, the secondary impulses are so well developed that they blot out the impact of the primary, or reflex impulse, a habit has formed. Habits are a necessary part of being able to function: Many are helpful (how to tie a shoelace or use a knife and fork), and some are chosen consciously (what route to take to work every day; a shower in the morning or a bath at night), but most mental and emotional habits ("I never cry," "I always think that . . . ," "I can't sing," "I always cry when they play the national anthem") are formed unconsciously and by people other than oneself, in childhood. There is no choice attached to such conditioning. Behavior that is suggested or demanded from outside develops the ability to respond to secondary impulses rather than primary ones. "Stop that screaming or you get no ice cream." "Shut up or I'll spank you, you noisy little beast." Or, in extreme cases, "Take that; that'll teach you." "Sssh . . . you mustn't giggle in church, God is looking at you." "Big boys don't cry." "Nice little girls don't shout." "That's not funny; that's rude."

The animal instinct level of emotional response to stimulus, deep in the unconscious mind, is largely conditioned out of us as we grow up. There should be a balance of conscious control and instinctual response in mature behavior, but so much human behavior is unconsciously controlled by habits conditioned in childhood by arbitrary influences such as parents (or lack of them), teachers, peers or fellow gang members, movie stars, pop stars, that if we come to a point in our lives where we want access to the primitive sources of laughter, sorrow, anger, joy (as an actor must), they may seem to have been civilized or brutalized out of us. Throughout the nervous system impulses have been blocked, rerouted or crisscrossed with countermanding impulses.

In step (1) of How the Voice Works there is an example illustrating "the need to communicate," but even that need cannot be taken for granted. The ability to receive a stimulus may be impaired to the point that the exchange of greetings is a one-way trade. Assuming it does occur, however, responding to "good morning" may be subject to secondary impulses such as "Why is he talking to me? He doesn't usually say a word." Or "What's that funny bruise on her forehead?" Or "I know, you're going to ask me to sign a petition," etc. This interrupts the voyage of electrical impulse to breathing and laryngeal musculature, and sends a second electrical impulse to hold on to the breathing muscles so that they will not react spontaneously. The breathing muscles fail to deliver the natural fuel of breath to the vocal folds, but the necessity of replying remains, so a little breath is found under the collarbone, just enough to activate vibration, while the muscles of the throat, jaw, lips and tongue work twice as hard to compensate for the lack of breath power. The resultant tone is thin, and the message it carries is noncommittal. That is one way, out of a thousand more subtle ones, of avoiding a spontaneous response.

It is not that spontaneity is right and calculation is wrong, but that spontaneity should be possible, and it seldom is. This is because certain neuro-muscular programming has developed habits of mind and muscle that cut us off from the instinctual connection between emotion and breath. The voice cannot work to its true potential if its basic energy is not breath. As long as we are emotionally protective our breathing cannot be free. As long as breath is not free the voice will depend on compensating strength in the throat and mouth muscles. When these muscles try to convey strong feelings a number of possible results can occur: they find a safe, musical way to describe emotion; they drive sound monotonously up into the head; or they tense, contract, push and squeeze with so much effort that the vocal folds rub together. Then the folds become inflamed, lose their resilience, are unable to produce regular vibrations and finally, grow little lumps on them as they grind against each other without the lubrication of breath. Then all that is heard is a gritty, hoarse sound and, ultimately, nothing.

It is easy to see how step (5) "the vibrations are amplified by resonators" can be interfered with by the same inhibitory messages that confuse steps (1) to (4).

There are some constructive interferences that create harmonics and enrich the sound with complexities, but before those can be relied on, the interferences that restrict range and resonance must be removed. Some of these are the direct result of the problems that arise when breathing is restricted. If the throat is tense with effort, it constricts the channel through which sound travels. Most commonly this constriction prevents the vibrations from traveling freely down into the lower resonating chambers of the pharynx and chest, restricting amplification to the middle and upper resonators. This can result in a light, high or strident tone. Sometimes throat tension, coupled with an unconscious need to sound manly or in control, can push the larynx down so that the sound *only* resonates in the lower cavities, and a monotonously rich, deep voice is developed that cannot find light and shade from the upper part of the range. If the soft palate and back of the tongue have joined the battalion of substitutes for breath, they may bunch together with muscular effort and drive the voice up into the nose rather than allow it free passage between them into the mouth. The nasal resonator is powerful, dominating and unsubtle. If the voice settles in the nose, there is little difficulty being heard, but *what* is heard may not be what is intended. Nuance is ironed out, and variety of thought cannot find free play through a corresponding variety of resonating qualities. Content is distorted by the one resonating form available.

These are three of the most obvious distorted resonating reactions that can occur when the voice is not free. More subtly, the whole tuning apparatus is subject to any messages sent from the mind that tighten the body. If the breathing muscles tense, so does the muscle tissue lining the pharynx. As those tiny muscles tighten in response to inhibitory messages, they can no longer perform their subtle movements, tightening and releasing in response to the constantly changing pitches of thought inflection, thereby regulating the aperture through which sound flows and amplifying its changing pitches. Such muscle tension diminishes the ability of the voice to be inflected directly by thought.

Voice inflections can also be manipulated by the ear and conscious muscular control but as the manipulative skill increases, so does the distance from the truth.

By step (6), "the resultant sound is articulated by the lips and tongue to form words," it may seem that everything has gone so far wrong that communication is impossible. Indeed, the lips and tongue may now be responsible for so many duties abdicated by the breath and resonators (as they fall victim to tension), that their simple articulative ability is buried under the burden. It is certain that until the tongue can relax while basic sound is being formed, it cannot easily perform its natural function, which is to mold that sound. The tongue is attached to the larynx (by the hyoid bone), and the larynx communicates directly with the diaphragm through the trachea. Tension in one of these three areas causes tension in the other two. As long as there is tension in the tongue it will articulate with more effort than necessary, thereby diminishing its sensitivity of response to motor impulses from the speech cortex.

Whereas the tongue seems more intimately connected with the inner workings of the vocal apparatus and subject to the same tensions, the lips reflect a slightly different aspect of those inhibitions. They are part of the complex facial musculature which responds to inhibitory messages from the mind by drawing a curtain across the window of the face. The face can be the most or the least revealing part of the body. Some faces harden into impassive masks behind which their owners can calculate, plan and maintain invulnerability; others assume the mask of appeasment – the muscles of a cajoling smile gradually programming a permanent upward slant; others have fallen into such heavy dejection that a moment of optimism can hardly lift the corners of the mouth. It is perfectly normal for facial posture to reveal the emphatic parts of a personality formed in the course of forty or fifty years. In the early years those muscles can be prevented from setting prematurely by allowing them to pick up the complexities of changing moods and responses. This is natural exercise for these muscles that, like other muscles of the body, become flaccid or stiff without exercise. For this to happen though, people must want to reveal themselves, be unafraid of such openness of countenance and believe that "vulnerability is strength."

The lips, as the part of the face that guards the mouth, can develop into heavily armed portcullises or doors on well-oiled hinges which open readily to allow egress. The stiff upper lip is no mere symbol of British phlegm; it exists commonly, and seems to stiffen in response to a determined need not to show fear or doubt. It can also stiffen simply to hide bad teeth or a smile that its owner thought unattractive in formative years. The freedom of the top lip is essential to lively articulation. Articulating responsibility should be equally divided between the top lip and the bottom lip to achieve maximum efficiency. If the top lip is stiff, the bottom lip will be doing at least 85% of the work and will probably enlist the jaw as extra support. The jaw is very clumsy compared with a lip, and articulation cannot be economical in such a situation.

It would take a whole book to chart the brilliant deviations the voice can take to prevent its owner from being known. There are voices which have grown expert in proclaiming a hard, aggressive go-getter in order to shield a frightened, insecure little boy; voices which sigh out wispily to disguise the strength of a woman who unconsciously knows that in a man's world she must pretend weakness to achieve anything; voices which are rich and relaxed and deep, signaling confidence and accomplishment where nothing is being done. The false voice can be tuned to exquisite duplicity.

This chapter, however, is intended only as a negative introduction to a positive book, dedicated to the voice that will transparently reveal the truth about its owner, if the owner so wishes.

Here is a summary of some negative factors and their effect on the voice:

I. Breathing

A. Effects of emotion on breathing (such as, protective neuro-muscular responses which inhibit the free flow of breath)

B. Postural habits (such as a sunken chest which inhibits intercostal breathing, or a sway-back which inhibits diaphragmatic freedom)

C. Control of breathing through the large outside muscles which denies the sensitivity of the involuntary nervous system control

II. Vocal folds and larynx

Lack of freedom in the breathing shifts too much responsibility for sound making to the delicate laryngeal muscles. These muscles are not equipped to deal with it, and consequently they tighten and destroy the free play of the vocal folds.

III. Resonating system

A. Tension in the larynx and throat blocks the voice from the pharyngeal and chest resonators, thereby inhibiting the lower register.

B. Tension in the back of the tongue, soft palate, face and neck hinders the free use of the mask and head resonators, thereby inhibiting the middle and upper registers.

IV. Articulating system

When the breath is not free to support the sound, the tongue provides compensatory strength, diminishing its role in articulation. Habitual psychological tensions are often reflected in tight lips, whose articulating ability is impaired.

*   *   *

Lest this chapter present a daunting prospect of work to be accomplished, it should be emphasized, now and continually, that clear thinking and free emotional expression help tremendously in solving the problems. A psycho-physical approach is a perfect example of the conundrum, "Which came first, the chicken or the egg?", but the following two maxims should underlie all work on the voice:

Muddy thinking is the fundamental obstacle to clear articulation.

Blocked emotions are the fundamental obstacle to a free voice.

Part one:
The freeing process

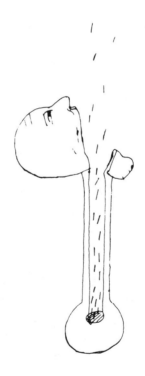

3: The spine:
the support of breath

The first step toward freeing the natural voice is to develop an ability to perceive habits and register new experiences. Such ability must be mental and physical, and the perception eventually refined to extreme subtlety in order to observe the minutiae of neuro-muscular behavior that serves the need to communicate. It is fruitless to demand such subtlety in the beginning since few people have immediate capacity for fine psycho-physical awareness; carefully graded steps must be taken to arrive at a state which can be trusted to feed back reliable information.

The first exercise will be useless if you read quickly through the instructions and realize that the resultant movements are to stretch and drop down the spine. It is a familiar exercise, and can be done quite mechanically, achieving some superficial release through the large external muscles of the body. But it is the process by which the stretch and the dropping down are arrived at that constitutes the exercise. It is generally true in all the exercises, that it is not *what* you are doing that is important, but *how* you are doing it. The conscious mind has an alarming capacity for subverting new experiences, either confusing them with something familiar and safe, or leaping ahead to the result and by-passing the process. For instance, to greet the sense of deep relaxation with the comment, "This is how I feel just before I go to sleep at night," reinforces the familiar equation of sleep and relaxation, successfully precluding a new possibility: that of relaxation generating energy. The overall aim of the work on the spine is to develop physical awareness through specific relaxation. As unnecessary knots of tension undo, they release trapped energy into the body, creating a lively state of awareness and potential mobility.

More specifically, you will find that the efficiency of the vocal apparatus depends on the alignment of the body and the economy with which it functions. When the spine is out of alignment its ability to support the body is diminished and muscles intended for other things must provide that support. If the lower spine is weak, the abdominal muscles supply substitute strength for the torso; if the abdominal muscles are employed in holding up the body, they are not free to respond to breathing needs. Similarly, if the upper part of the spine abandons its job of carrying the rib cage and shoulder girdle, the rib muscles may take on the responsibility of holding the chest high, in which case they are unavailable for intercostal breathing. Finally, when the vertebrae of the neck are not well aligned, the whole channel through which the voice travels is distorted. With a weak neck, the jaw muscles, tongue muscles, laryngeal muscles, even lips and eyebrows become supporters of the head, leaving little chance of a free passage for sound.

Moshe Feldenkrais says in his invaluable book, *Awareness Through Movement*:

> "Any posture is acceptable in itself as long as it does not conflict with the law of nature, which is that the skeletal structure should counteract the pull of gravity, leaving the muscles free for movement. The nervous system and the frame develop together under the influence of gravity in such a way that the skeleton will hold up the body without expending energy despite the pull of gravity. If, on the other hand, the muscles have to carry out the job of the skeleton, not only do they use energy needlessly, but they are prevented from carrying out their main function of changing the position of the body, that is, of movement."

The first step, then, in freeing the voice, *is getting acquainted with your spine.*

The more you can imagine the movements in terms of the skeleton, the more economically the muscles will work. Let your mind talk to your bones.

STEP 1   ■ *Stand easily with your feet six or eight inches apart.*
Be aware of your weight evenly distributed over both feet; be aware that you are balanced equally between your toes and your heels.
In your mind's eye picture the bones of your feet.

Picture the shin bones growing up from your ankle joints.

Picture your thigh bones growing up from your knee joints.

Picture your hip joints and the pelvic girdle.

Picture your spine growing up from the pelvic girdle, through the small of the back, between the shoulder blades, with the rib cage floating round it and the shoulder girdle on top.

Feel the arms hanging from the shoulder sockets.

Picture the upper arm bones, the elbow joints, the forearms, the wrist joints, the bones of the hands and fingers. Let your mind flow back up through your arms and into the neck.

Picture the neck vertebrae going up into the skull.

Picture the skull floating, like a balloon, off the top of the spine.

STEP 2   ■ Focus your attention into your elbow joints, and let them float gently up toward the ceiling. This should involve the upper arms only — no shoulder muscles, no forearm muscles, no hand muscles.

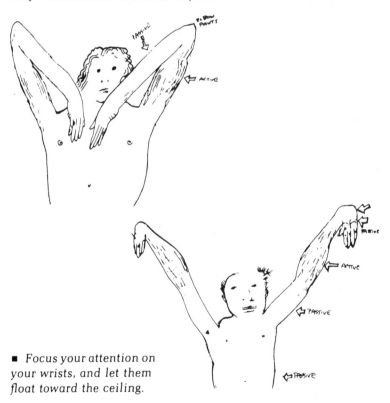

■ Focus your attention on your wrists, and let them float toward the ceiling.

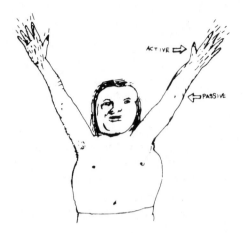

ACTIVE ⇨

⇦ PASSIVE

■ Focus your attention on your finger tips, and let them float to the ceiling.

Imagine someone pulls you up a little by your finger tips, and allow your whole torso to be stretched from above; leave your legs out of the stretch.

■ Now do one thing and one thing only: Let your hands relax until they hang from your wrists.

Register the contrasting sensations in your hands and in your arms.

Now let your forearms relax until they hang loose from the elbows.

Register the contrasting sensations in the forearms and hands, and in the upper arms and shoulders.

Now let the arms drop heavily, to hang loosely from the shoulders.

Register the weight of the arms, the blood running back into the hands, the temperature changes.

Now let the weight of the head drop heavily forward so that the head and neck hang off the top of the torso.

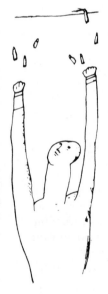

The fingertips float toward the ceiling.

■ Feel the weight of the head dragging on the spine, and gradually give in to the weight, so that the spine undoes, giving in to gravity, vertebra by vertebra, from the top down. Try to picture the vertebrae one by one.

Let your knees relax so that the weight remains over the middle of the feet.

Check that your weight does not rock back on your heels, or forward on your toes. Check that your knees do not lock. When the weight is too much to support through balance, release the spine quickly, and hang upside down.

Imagine your torso is hanging from your tailbone, giving in to the force of gravity.

Breathe easily. You are doing this to relax all the torso muscles, shoulder muscles, neck muscles, head and arms.

■ *Now focus your attention on your tailbone and, from there, begin to build the spine up again, vertebra by vertebra, as though building a castle of nursery bricks one on top of the other.*

Do not use the stomach muscles; leave them hanging loose; breathe.

Do not suddenly straighten the knees; let them gradually straighten as the balance shifts.

Find the vertebrae that lift the rib cage, and build them up from the small of the back. You are now an upright, headless torso.

Focus on the top seven vertebrae that make up the neck, and gradually build them up on top of the rest of the spine. Be aware that the head floats up as a result of the neck build. You do not "lift your head."

STEP 3

You are now an upright headless torso.

■ *Let your mind travel from your feet, up through your legs, to the torso, and consciously relax any muscles that begin to tighten in the stomach, buttocks, shoulders, neck. You are actively transferring the energy needed to remain upright from the large, external muscles of the body, to an internal picture of the spine constantly working against the force of gravity. It is as though the spine is a stream of upward-moving energy, fueled by the mind.*

■ *Be aware of the shape your body cuts in the air.*

■ *Be aware of the feeling of air touching your skin.*

■ *Now, closing your eyes, turn your attention inward and become aware of your body from inside, for one or two minutes.*

■ *Stretch, yawn, shake your body all over.*

STEP 4

It is good to do this sequence with your eyes closed, so, if you are working on your own, read the following instructions through before starting.

■ *Standing easily, with a sense of the spine moving upward, supporting the torso, close your eyes again. With the purpose of relaxing the inner muscles of your body, let your mind's eye travel from the inside of the top of your skull down the inside of the mask of your face, down through your throat, down through your chest.*

Notice the tiny, inevitable movement of your breathing as you move your mind down into the stomach, down through the intestines and lower stomach into the groin. Undo any holding tensions you find inside. Keep the spine moving upward as you relax the muscles around it or you will collapse.

- *Allow the whole of the inside of the torso to be available to the movement of your breath.*

Observe the reaction of the inside of your body to the involuntary movements of your breathing apparatus.

Then, deep inside, feel the need to yawn and stretch; begin to yield to that need.

Yawn, stretch, shake out your body as though getting up in the morning, or as a dog yawns, stretches, then shakes his skin back into place on the bones:

- *Register how your body feels; register how you feel.*

In the course of this exercise you have made conscious decisions about how your physical energy is to be deployed. If you have followed the process in detail, both mentally and physically, you will have dislodged a few habitual muscle responses. You should have experienced quite clearly the contrasting sensations of relaxation and tension in parts of the body that are relatively easy to contact. This experience is the basis for developing the ability to notice tensions in more inaccessible parts of the body (such as the back of the tongue, the center of the diaphragm, the upper lip), and to be able to release them.

The ability to relax must be cultivated slowly and with specific intent, otherwise it degenerates into the state of general collapse that Jerzy Grotowski rightly disparaged: "One cannot be completely relaxed as is taught in many theatre schools, for he who is totally relaxed is nothing more than a wet rag." There is, however, a vital difference between relaxing for the sake of relaxation, which inevitably includes mental collapse, and relaxing in order to do something. The aim is to remove unnecessary tensions so that the muscles are free to respond to impulse, without the short-circuiting created by habit.

. . . nothing more than a wet rag

4: Breathing:
the source of sound

Having reached a state of some awareness and relaxation through exploring the spine, it is now possible to begin to explore the breathing process. The complexities of the breathing machinery are such that it is wise not to jump to any conclusions about how it works at this juncture. Instead, begin to develop the ability to *observe without controlling*. The aim is to remove habitual muscular controls and allow the involuntary processes to take over. It is quite possible for the conscious mind to become aware of the function of the involuntary nervous system without interfering, but it is an unfamiliar activity. The tendency may be to observe, correctly, that when you breathe in, your stomach moves out, and when you breathe out your stomach goes in, and to use that observation to start controlling the breath with the stomach muscles. You might start to pull your stomach in, which blows the breath out, and to push your stomach out, which draws the breath in. This is a misuse of perception. The involuntary breathing muscles are subtle, complex, powerful and deep inside the body. Any voluntary controls that you apply will involve muscles that are large, clumsy, external, and at several removes from the lungs. Conscious control of the breath will destroy its sensitivity to changing inner states, and severely curtail the reflex connection of breathing and emotional impulse. It is worth repeating here the warning that *you cannot imitate a reflex action*. Natural breathing is reflexive, and the only work you can do to restore its potential is to remove restrictive tensions and provide it with a diversity of stimuli.

These stimuli will provoke deeper and stronger reflex actions than are normally exercised in habit-run daily lives.

It is a good idea to start the observation of your breathing in a standing position so that later you may benefit by contrasting observations when you lie down or hang upside down.

STEP 1 ■ *Repeat the physical awareness spine exercises in Chapter 3.*

STEP 2 ■ *Standing easily, with a long spine, relaxed muscles and your mind centered in the middle of your body, allow your involuntary breathing rhythm to tell you what it is.*

Consciously, all you can do is keep releasing tension from the stomach area, the shoulders and the lower belly, and be aware of the breath apparently moving your body, rather than your body moving the breath. Remember that your natural breathing rhythm may not be your familiar breathing rhythm.

■ *Explore the following description of the breathing process: The outgoing breath is complete inner relaxation. The incoming breath will happen automatically if you wait.*

STEP 3 ■ *Let the breath release out of you.*
Wait – but don't hold the muscles – until you feel the need for a new breath.
Yield to the need.
Let the breath be replaced (do not "breathe in").

Let the breath release again.
Relax into a small internal pause.
As soon as you feel, deep inside, the tiny impulse of need, give in to it, and allow the new breath in.

■ *Repeat the mental processes of Step 3, observing the physical reactions:*

■ *Release the breath out.*
Wait.
Allow the breath in.
Release the breath out.
Wait.
Allow the breath in.
Release the breath out.
Wait.
Allow the breath in . . . etc.

These breaths are on a tiny scale, very central, and are sufficient to keep you alive from one moment to the next. The more relaxed you are, the smaller the exchange of oxygen necessary to sustain you. It is worth noting that in deep meditation breathing slows down radically, and sometimes is barely perceptible. Anxiety and tension either speed up the breathing rate, or slow it down laboriously, or dictate a longer, heavier exchange.

STEP 4   ■ *Continue the breathing awareness found in Step 3 and let your mouth drop open so that you are breathing through your mouth, not through your nose. Don't open wide, just enough to allow the breath to pass through.*

If your mouth is relaxed, the breath should automatically arrive in a small "fff" somewhere between the top teeth and the lower lip.

■ *Don't make a "fff" sound; let it be the natural by-product of the release of breath from inside and the relaxed position of the mouth.*

According to individual mouths, the "fff" may occur more obviously between the two lips rather than the teeth and lower lip; the important point is, that with the small "fff" you begin to program the breath to release from the center of the body and arrive in the front of the mouth, which is what happens with a free sound. All breathing awareness exercises are blueprints for sound; it is therefore essential that all breathing exercises should be done with the mouth open, as it is when speaking. In repose, or when walking in the street, it is aesthetically and hygienically practical to breathe through the nose, which serves to clean, filter and moisten the air on its long, relatively slow passage to the lungs. For speaking, the breath must be able to respond quickly to fast-changing impulse, and the direct, wide passage through the mouth is clearly needed. If you open the mouth too wide, however, the breath will arrive most obviously in the throat rather than the front of the mouth, making a "hhhhh" rather than a "fffff." This programs a route for sound which also emphasizes the throat, and is not free.

In practicing the breathing awareness exercises, it is vital to realize the difference between saying "the breath should be in the front of the mouth, so I will put it there," and "the breath will arrive in the front of the mouth if it is released freely from inside and there is no tension on the way out which holds it back." It is necessary to condition the mind to be interested primarily in the causal, release point, not the resultant, arrival point.

STEP 5   ■ *Continue the awareness of your natural breathing rhythm.*

Mouth just open, small *"ffff"* 's on each outgoing breath.

Feel that your breath and your observing mind are both in the same place: the center of your body. Make sure that you are not split in two, with part of you sitting up in your head, commenting from above. You and your breathing are one and the same thing. When your breath releases, you release.

■ *Now feed into your middle the impulse for a gentle sigh of relief. No sound.*

Observe how your breathing reacts to the stimulus of a simple easy feeling of relief

You will find that more breath comes in, in response to the impulse, and that more breath releases out, on a longer *"ffffff"* as the relief pours out.

■ *Again consciously decide to feel a sigh of relief. Consciously observe the reaction in the involuntary breathing musculature.*

■ *Imagine that your mind (the impulse-dispatcher), your feelings (impulse-receiver), and your breath are all in the same place: the center of your body.*

■ *Again feed in the impulse to sigh with relief.*

Feel the relief deep inside your body.

Release the relief and the breath as one.

Relax inside. Allow the breath to be replaced.

You can affect the breathing musculature, provoke it to greater efforts, but do not confuse the consciousness of emotional control, through the application of emotional impulses, with conscious muscular control.

STEP 6   ■ *Make it all easy now by lying flat on your back on the floor and observing the breathing processes in a position where no energy is being expended on remaining upright. All the attention can now go into noticing how the breathing works when the body is fully relaxed.*

■ *Lying on your back, let your whole body give in to gravity.*

■ *Send your mind into the soles of your feet and think of relaxing your toes and feet so that they appear to drop away from your ankles.*

Imagine your ankle joints are filled with air.

Let your calf muscles relax so that the flesh, skin and muscles seem to dissolve off the shinbones.

Imagine your knee joints are filled with air.

Let your thigh muscles relax so that the flesh, skin and muscles seem to dissolve off the thigh bones.

Imagine your hip joints and thigh sockets are filled with air so that the legs do not seem to be attached to the torso. Let your buttock muscles, pelvic muscles, groin and lower belly muscles dissolve and melt.

Be aware of your spine giving in to gravity from the tailbone to the skull.

Let the small of the back relax, but realize that there is a natural curve there — don't try to flatten it out.

Let the whole stomach area melt, dissolve, relax.

Picture the part of the back that is between the shoulder blades spreading away from the spine to either side.

Imagine the rib bones as soft as the belly: Let them give in to gravity and release into breath.

Picture the torso as releasing into length and breadth along and across the floor.

■ Imagine your shoulder sockets are filled with air, so that your arms seem to be hardly attached to the torso.

Be aware of the weight of your arms and hands, heavy and abandoned on the floor.

Be aware of your fingers.

■ Let your attention travel back up your arms, through your shoulders and into your neck.

Let your neck-spine give in to gravity, but realize there is a natural curve in these top seven vertebrae — don't try to flatten it.

Let your throat relax.

Feel the weight of your head on the floor.

■ Let the jaw muscles relax right beside the ears so that your teeth are not clenched.

Let the tongue relax inside the mouth so that it is not clamped to the roof of the mouth.

Be aware of your face muscles and let them melt so that the skin of the face feels heavy on the bones.

Let the cheeks go and the lips, the forehead, the eyelids.

Let the scalp muscles relax.

- Now let your attention sweep back down through your whole body, abandoned on the floor.

Imagine you could melt down through the floor.

Take a little time to enjoy this sensation.

Now become aware that in the middle of the stillness of your completely relaxed body, there is an inevitable, easy rise and fall as your breath enters and leaves you.

Feel the cool air being drawn in from outside through your nose or mouth, traveling down to the center of your torso, and being released from there, warm, to escape again to the outside.

Flop a hand onto the breathing area so that you can feel from outside what is happening inside.

Notice that on the outgoing breath, the area under your hand can fall straight toward the ground.

Feed a deep sigh of relief far down into your body – imagine the relief going right down into the groin – and let the feeling fall out of you with abandon.

Here, you are enlisting the aid of gravity to increase the possibility of complete muscular release on the outgoing breath. The whole belly area should be able to drop suddenly, without controls, with much the same quality of release that happens if you lift your arm off the floor and then let it relax completely, giving in suddenly to gravity. You can test the mind's willingness to relinquish physical control of breathing, by asking it to hand the process over to the pull of gravity. Until you can remove all controls, there is no way of choosing controls when necessary; you are still prey to unconscious habitual controls.

The exercise, therefore, is:

- *Feed in the relief (causal impulse).*

Let it fly out of you uncensored by controls (resultant communication).

- *Observe that a deeper sigh of relief stimulates a larger breath experience.*

Observe that the impulse moves the breath and the breath moves the body.

If you think along these lines you are less likely to add extra effort to the economical work performed by the involuntary nervous system.

- *Explore varying degrees of strength in causal impulse feeding into the breathing center; from natural breathing, to a small, contented*

*sigh, to a larger, grateful sigh, to a huge, deep sigh of relief (imagine
something bad was going to happen, but was averted).*

Relax back to natural breathing.

STEP 7 ■ *Slowly, with complete physical awareness, get up from the floor
to a standing position.*

*See how much you can retain of the physical sensations you experi-
enced while on the floor, for instance:*

Imagine that the floor is still supporting your back.

*Leave your stomach muscles as sloppy as they were when you were
lying down.*

*Imagine the force of gravity is behind you and let the stomach wall
fall with it on the outgoing breath.*

Observe the natural rhythm of your breathing.

*Observe any differences between breathing lying down and standing
up.*

*Observe any differences there may be between your breathing now
and the last time you were aware of it while standing.*

*Know what you are experiencing not in terms of right and wrong but
in terms of change.*

Where, specifically, in your body do you feel movement in response
to breath? In your ribs? Back? Sides? Belly? Groin? Internally? Externally?

What feels better than before? What feels worse? How do you feel?

Where is the breath releasing from? Where is it going?

Do you feel more awake? Do you feel sleepy? Do you feel confused?

Have you found anything new?

I will not provide any answers to these questions. It is important that
each person who is working on self in this particular field keeps asking such questions, and answers with a growing knowledge of what
is true in the individual, organic experience.

The difficulty, in working on oneself, is to admit new experiences.
Most of us have considerable investment in our conditioning because it has gotten us this far already, is reasonably reliable and is
safe. If you can ask yourself, from the start, questions about the *new*
sensations you have experienced, and even make it an exercise to articulate your answers in specific terms out loud, you will learn and
change twice as fast. As has been pointed out before, the mind is re-

luctant to embrace deep change, and will play devious games to maintain the status quo. We are dealing with functions that should be automatic and it takes great determination to change habits programmed at this level. In these exercises the new experiences are on a deeper level of consciousness than your everyday level; when you verbalize the experience you bring it up to a more familiar level of consciousness and the new experience becomes reinforced, making a firmer imprint.

Here is a scene enacted, with variations, quite often in the course of voice classes I have taught, which shows some of the ways the mind escapes change.

The pupil has been taken through the work described in this and the previous chapter, and it is visibly evident that the breathing is deeper in the body, freer, less labored.

Me: How do you feel?

Pupil: Fine. Good.

Me: What do you feel?

Pupil: I don't know exactly.

Me: Do you feel any differences?

Pupil: Not really. I feel dizzy, and a bit sick.

Me: What about your breathing? (Silence). Do you notice it affecting any new parts of your body?

Pupil: Oh, yes. It's much easier.

Me: Where?

Pupil: Wait a minute, I'll have to think back. Mmmmm — yes — well, I've never felt it in my lower back before. (Or stomach, or legs, it doesn't matter.)

Me: What do you feel happens there now?

Pupil: Well, it's sort of as though I breathe into my buttocks (Or pelvis, or knees, etc.).

Me: OK, fine.

Pupil: Is that right?

Me: If you feel it, then it's happened, and that's fine for the time being.

Pupil: But are you supposed to breathe in your ass?

We might then go on to discuss the fact that the lungs only go down as far as the diaphragm, which cuts the body in two, horizontally; that when breath goes in, the diaphragm moves down, pushing the stomach down, which in turn pushes the lower intestines down, so that there are graphic movements in the lower torso in response to breath. These movements are not confined to the front of the body, and the lower spine must be free of tension to allow full use of the breathing apparatus. It will then lengthen and shorten in response to large breathing demands, helping to create the greatest space possible inside the torso into which the lungs can expand. These spine movements are imperceptible when standing, but can easily be observed when lying face downwards.

The important thing in badgering the pupil about what had happened in the course of the exercise was to find even one specific point in the general experience which could be articulated and therefore learned both organically and consciously. The diversionary tactics employed by the pupil's mind to avoid coping with something new were, roughly as follows: The first answer, "fine — good," hopes that I will be flattered by the success of the exercise and leave him alone. Secondly, "I don't know" can be interpreted as "let me enjoy my subjective experience which is private, personal and will be spoiled if I talk about it"; it is generally resistant. Thirdly, "I will not admit change for the better; I will concentrate on this rather unpleasant, disoriented, dizzy feeling." It is very natural to feel a bit dizzy (a) on standing up after lying on the floor for some time, because of the alteration in the balance mechanism, and (b) because, with deep relaxation, more oxygen begins to enter and leave the body, stimulating circulation and pumping more blood to the heart and the brain. This is a healthy situation, but until the body adjusts to the newness of it, there may be some dizziness. As this is quite a common experience, and one that sometimes causes alarm, I will digress for a moment on that subject.

If you can learn to accept dizziness when it occurs, you will not be sick; though you may feel it, you will not fall down; you may feel you are about to fall but you will find you can embrace the state as a useful disorientation out of which you can explore a new use of yourself. If, however, you are frightened by the dizziness you *may* throw up, you *can* faint and, by so doing, you will have successfully used it to escape from a new experience. The release of tension in some extremely nervous people, and the consequent submission of the lungs to the powerful involuntary nervous system, can be such a turnover in the whole state of being that dizziness is a way of life for a time. Once such people have fainted a couple of times, they become familiar with the process and find the moment when they can choose to go with it and regularly pass out, or focus on something more interesting such as the exercise in hand. This may sound callous but without such confrontation, significant change and growth can be postponed forever. It should also be emphasized that it is not necessary to faint in order to liberate your breathing.

In this chapter the initial attitude to the breathing process that has been suggested is that the involuntary nervous system does it best. That, if you allow the breathing to tell you what it wants, you do not have to waste energy controlling or sustaining it consciously. That, the ultimate controls for the breath are thoughts and feelings. That, instead of sending active messages to yourself, such as "breathe in," "breathe out," "take a breath," "inhalation," "exhalation," you send passive messages such as "allow the breath to replace," "let the breath release," "let the breath drop in," or "fall out"; "incoming breath" and "outgoing breath." It takes longer in the beginning, but once reprogrammed, you will find the newly found *natural* way much more efficient than anything you could devise.

5: The touch of sound

An unremitting effort will be made, in this and subsequent chapters, to shift the job of judging sound from the aural to the tactile sense. As long as work on the voice includes listening to sounds to check their quality, there will be a conditioned split between the head and the heart, and emotion will be censored by intellect rather than shaped by it. By the "touch" of sound, I mean the feeling of vibrations in the body, and initially that sound will be explored as another inhabitant of that central part of the body already housing breath, feelings and impulses. The impetus for sound is impulse, and the raw material is breath; in order to remove effort from the throat, it helps to imagine that sound, as well as breath, starts from the middle of the body. Be prepared for a powerful application of your imagination in this. People tend to be conditioned to an unconscious physical sense that they communicate from just behind the face. Here you will be challenged to find a communicating center a good eighteen inches lower than expected.

STEP 1 ■ *Stand easily with an awareness of a long spine moving up the middle of the back, carrying the weight of the torso off the legs. Let your stomach muscles relax.*

You must sacrifice your vanity for a little while by abandoning a slim profile in the interest of inner relaxation. Really let your stomach sag, without becoming swaybacked or letting your knees lock.

■ *Keep sending two messages:*
"Lengthen the spine." "Let the muscles go."

■ *Tune in to your natural, everyday breathing, deep inside your body.*
Induce a sigh of relief.
Be aware of the breath responding and releasing through the mouth on an easy loose "fffff."
Feel that the breath is relief and the relief is breath. See if you can feel relief and breath affecting you in the lower half of the torso, from the diaphragm down.

■ *Now imagine that there is a pool of vibrations in the lower half of the torso.*

This time the sigh of relief is going to find vibrations to release on instead of breath.

■ *Leave the mouth loosely open.*
Feed in the impulse for a sigh of relief — deep down into the pool of vibrations.
Sigh the relief out on a stream of vibrations.
Relax inside, and allow the breath to replace.

As the mouth is only a little bit open, and quite relaxed, the resultant sound will be a continuous, rather formless "hu-u-u-uh." (Similar to an English "her," the American "her" before the R changes the vowel, or some American pronunciations of the vowel sound in "hut." I shall be spelling it "huh.") If the mouth opens wider, the sound becomes more like "haa-aa" in "father"; if the mouth is not relaxed enough to drop open easily, three-quarters of the sound will go into the nose. The sound is the primitive, unformed, neutral one that happens when there is no tension in the throat or mouth to distort it, and no vowel demand to mold it.

■ *Explore sighing relief out on the vibrations of sound.*
Imagine that the source of feeling and vibration is deep inside the body, and that nothing impedes the "huh" sound as it sighs through the mouth into the outside air.
Make sure that the relief connects with 100% vibrations, not 50% breath and 50% vibrations.

This is general work to focus the mind, and to begin to experience a connection between sound vibrations and feeling that is physical.
    In Step 2 you will be looking for a more precise and sensitive

touch of sound. This involves a specific picture of the diaphragm as the most central and initial point of connection between the breath and the sound. Try to focus on not only the diaphragm, but the center point of the diaphragm. You cannot feel the diaphragm, but by picturing it, you can sharpen and sensitize the mind's connection with sound.

You will find in the following three illustrations an idea of how the diaphragm moves as breath goes in and out. In repose, the diaphragm is dome-shaped; a large muscle, attached at its circumference to the bottom of the rib cage, and to the breast bone in front. It cuts the whole body in two, horizontally.

When breath comes in, the diaphragm moves downward, flattening. When breath goes out, the diaphragm moves upward, the dome becoming more cone-shaped. (The downward movement is contraction, and the upward one expansion, but this is one of the scientific facts that only serves to confuse the lay practitioner and is best ignored.)

Before moving to Step 2, practice the sigh of relief with the picture of your torso as an expanding and contracting cylinder, and your diaphragm as an elastic, rubbery shelf being blown down by the incoming breath, and up by the outgoing breath. The picture applies to the large effect of a sigh impulse; obviously the movements are infinitely more subtle for ordinary breathing.

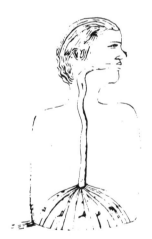 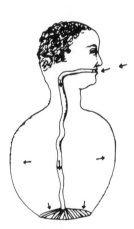 

Repose
a dome shaped diaphragm.

Incoming breath
the diaphragm descends.

Outgoing breath
diaphragm rises.

STEP 2 ■ *Visualize a point at the very center of the dome of the diaphragm which responds to the tiny in and out of everyday breathing.*
Practice small "ffff"s in the rhythm of natural breathing with this

picture of the center of the dome of the diaphragm as the starting point of breath.

■ *Now visualize touching vibrations that already exist inside you, sensitively and precisely with that central point. The sound will be "huh."*

Stay within the rate and rhythm of your natural breathing.

Instead of "fff" on the outgoing breath there is now a small "huh" sound.

Touch the vibrations lightly "huh" and leave them.

Breath will automatically drop back in.

Touch again "huh" : relax and the breath will drop back in.

Repeat : within the ordinary rhythm of your natural breathing.

Now visualize
touching vibrations.

It is a small sound, and a small exchange of breath.

■ *Now let there be a double bounce of vibrations "huh-huh," still in the rhythm of natural breathing.*

Touch sound in the center of the diaphragm
    huh huh
Wait for the breath to want to replace, then yield to that need
    breath goes in ∅*
Touch sound
    huh huh
Relax inside
    breath goes in ∅
Touch sound
    huh huh
Relax
    breath replaces
    huh huh
    ∅
    huh huh ∅ huh huh ∅ huh huh ∅

* This ∅ will be the symbol for a new breath

Just explore the physical sensation of sound in the center of the torso. The physical sensation of the breathing should remain as close as possible to the sensation there is when you are breathing naturally without sound. Try not to make the sound; try to let it be the by-product of the "touch" picture, in the same way that you do not make light in an electric bulb; you press a switch, or put a plug in a socket, and light happens. The analogy is exact. Let sound happen. You are practicing dealing with cause and letting effect follow.

It may be hard to prevent your muscles from helping to make the sound at this point. It may seem that the sound still centers in your throat however much you try to visualize it lower down. In order to remove excess effort, do the same exercise lying flat on your back on the floor.

As you relax more and more, you should find that your abdominal wall can give in to gravity, and that both your picture and the sensation of sound happening deeper in your body will clarify.

■ *Sigh with relief on sound, and as you sigh out, jiggle your loose belly with your hands so that the sound gets shaken manually.*

Imagine you are massaging the actual vibrations inside your belly, so that you become more and more familiar with the feeling of the vibrations being there rather than in your throat or your mouth.

■ *Then, go back to the central, sensitive touch of sound on*

   huh huh
   $\varnothing$
   huh huh
   $\varnothing$

■ *With the same sensitivity and clear picture of the central connection with sound, count one to five.*

   Say your name.
   Describe how you feel.
   Say a poem.

■ *Do all with the awareness of the physical sensation of sound deep inside.*

STEP 3   ■ *Slowly get up.*
Stand easily.
Repeat all the touch of sound exercises noticing any changes.

STEP 4   ■ *Drop down your spine until you are hanging head downward and repeat all the touch of sound exercises, noticing carefully the adjustment that occurs in your picture of the diaphragm. Take advantage of the fact that it can be much looser in this position, as the force of gravity is helping it to relax on the outgoing breath.*

■ *Slowly build up the spine and repeat the whole process standing. Sigh of relief on sound ∅ jiggling the sound with your hands ∅ huh ∅ huh ∅ huh ∅ huh huh ∅ huh huh ∅ huh huh.*

The sounds should be gradually getting easier, freer, deeper in the body, more pleasurable.

Remember that we are only dealing here with the *source* of sound, so do not be alarmed if it all seems very deep and introverted and self-indulgent. It should be. The depth of the sound, in terms of pitch, is, at this stage, a result of both the breathing muscles and the laryngeal muscles relaxing. You are feeding in very low energy because the first steps are concerned with undoing tension. Relaxed vocal folds produce a low frequency of vibrations and a low sound.

It is vital that you cultivate a familiarity with the state of relaxation. If that state is practiced and easily available when little demand is being made, there is a chance you will be able to maintain a balance between necessary tensions and unnecessary ones when demand is increased. This is the road to achieving maximum effect with minimum effort. You haven't a chance of singing a high "C" or delivering a speech charged with emotional intensity without undue strain if you have not mastered relaxation while exploring deep, easy, low-energy sound.

There is a deliberate emphasis on turning attention inward at this stage. This is to condition you to work causally, which, in the case of the voice, means feeding the source of sound, building the need to communicate, accumulating inner energy so that speaking will be a release. There is no point in developing a vocal instrument that performs dutifully, but has nothing it must say.

6: Vibrations that amplify the initial sound

Having established a working picture of the vibrations of sound originating in the middle of the body, we are now going to explore how they can be amplified and encouraged to grow. The next few exercises are based on two general ideas:

1. Vibrations are murdered by tension.
2. Vibrations thrive on having attention paid them.

To deal with (1), we shall isolate and eliminate pockets of muscle-tension that trap and stifle vibrations, while (2) depends first on recognizing vibrations when and where they occur, and then on nurturing them.

The nature of vibrations is to multiply, to re-sound, or resound. They reverberate off an infinite variety of sounding boards. The first of these sounding boards we shall work with is that formed when you close your lips. Vibrations, originating centrally, will resound on them.

STEP 1   ■ *Establish your connection with the central starting point of sound on "huh huh."*

Then, finding a pitch that is close to the sound you have just made, touch sound on pitch.

huh   huh

- *Then, sustain the sound, as though on a long sigh, still on pitch.*

- *Sigh with relief again, on pitch, and this time close your lips on the sound.*
Register the feeling of vibrations on your lips.
Open your lips still sustaining the sound.
Stop.
Relax inside, and let the breath replace ∅

Try to carry this exercise out purely through following the physical steps, letting the sound be a by-product. Don't let your mind get smart and figure out what the resultant sound is meant to be, thereby allowing you merely to repeat an old and familiar sound, rather than discovering a new set of physical sensations in which the *sound* of the sound is relatively unimportant.

- *Now let the pitch drop (just a little, a semitone). Sigh out huh-hu-u-u-uh on pitch picturing the vibrations streaming up from the middle of the body and out through the mouth.*
Close your lips gently on the vibrations.
Feel the vibrations on your lips as though they were gathering re-inforcements there.
Let your lips open and the sound will stream on out reinforced by the extra vibrations found on the sounding-board of the lips.
Relax inside, let the breath drop back in ∅
Repeat the process on several more pitches, going down, then up again to the easy mid-register pitch you started on.

The sound that happened when you closed your lips on the vibrations is commonly known as humming. Keep working with it, however, in terms of physical awareness. When I take a short cut and ask you to "hum" try not to respond mechanically with your familiar humming, but let the vibrations flow from the middle of the body, through the mouth: close your lips and let the vibrations gather reinforcements from the sounding-board of those lips.

huh- hummmmmuh ◌ huh- hummmmmuh ◌ huh- hummmmmuh ◌ etc.

There is nearly always some tension in the lips, either through undue effort or habit. Since one of our major premises for increasing vibrations in the voice is that tension murders vibration, the next step will be to see whether the lips can be induced to deliver more reverberation for sound through greater relaxation.

STEP 2 ■ *Blow air out through your lips so that they flutter.*

This is rather difficult to describe on paper, but horses do it in a relaxing way, babies do it, and small children do it with sound when they are pretending to be trucks and motor cars. It is not essential as an exercise, but it relaxes and stimulates the whole lip area, it wakens up dormant vibrations, it helps energize the sound in the very front of the mouth; it is also fun to do. So it is worth working out the movement, with and without sound. Here are a few introductory ideas and different ways of describing it if you are still in doubt.

1. Put your fingers into the corners of your mouth and stretch it sideways into a wide grimace. Let go suddenly and blow out through your lips, vibrating them with the air.

2. Put your index finger against your front teeth as though you were miming brushing your teeth. Let your lips relax completely so that they fall on your finger. As though you were going to hum, let vibration flow through your mouth.

Imagine the vibrations are toothpaste, your finger, a toothbrush, and brush your teeth up and down leaving the lips quite relaxed. Revert to a nursery state of playing with sounds between your finger, your lips and your teeth.

Retain the relaxation of the lips, remove the finger, and blow out through the lips with the vibrations. The resultant sound will start with a loose sort of "b" and then sputter or flutter into a vibration that lazily imitates that of a motor. Let this happen very loosely, as though your lips started in your cheeks, and feel the vibrations spread as far as possible over your face. It will probably tickle. Look in a mirror to make sure the corners of the lips are loose, not tucking in.

STEP 3 ■ *Blow out through the lips on vibration, this time on pitch (start with an easy, mid-register pitch); on the same breath bring the lips together in a hum then open the lips and let the vibrations escape.*

Here now, are the physical steps and physical awarenesses for the above exercise:

■ *Loosen up extra vibrations on the lips by blowing through them, gather those vibrations together on the lips where they touch each other, let the vibrations escape as the lips open.*

Sustain the exercise with a long drawn-out sigh of relief under it.

Relax inside, let the breath drop in to replace what has been used.

Repeat on descending and ascending pitches thus: (the following symbol will be used to represent "blowing out through the lips on vibration": βμμμ).

βμμμμμ   mmm   u-u-uh   ͵ʾ βμμμ   mmm u-u-uh ͵ʾ βμμμ mmm   uh
(loosen   gather escape   ͵ʾ loosen gather escape ͵ʾ etc.)

Take your time, don't hurry the ingoing breath, let the sequence of actions find their own pace and rhythm while you explore and become familiar with the vibrations.

STEP 4   ■ *Repeat Step 1, observing any changes in experience. You may, for instance, find that there are more vibrations naturally happening in the very front of the mouth. Move your lips around on the humming, as though savoring the taste of the vibrations before letting them escape.*

Vibrations thrive on having attention paid them.

■ *Become a connoisseur of vibrations.*
   Taste them.
   Spread them around your face.
   Luxuriate in them.
   Indulge them.

It is now necessary to explain such phrases as "sigh out the sound on pitch," "touch sound on pitch" and "sustain the sound on pitch." These are used to avoid a conditioned response to the word "sing." The immediate response for some people is "I can't sing" or "I'm tone deaf," while others respond by producing sound quite differently from the way in which they would produce a speaking sound. The word "sing" is too loaded to be used casually in the present basic work. At this stage there is no difference in the physical procedures necessary for speaking or singing. In singing you sustain a pitch, in speaking you come off the pitch immediately, employing quarter-tones, eighth-tones, even sixteenth-tones in inflection and intonation. At this point the whole emphasis in the work is on physical awareness, and it helps to have some variety while practicing the physical processes, hence the use of ascending and descending pitches. If you repeat an exercise only in your speaking voice you will tend to remain within your customary range and habitual patterns of inflection, never expanding into unknown areas. With the aid of varying pitch you can introduce new notes and a new range of tonal possibilities which will automatically liven up your speaking voice in ways you could not consciously plan.

Now that you are sustaining a sound through three phases, (touch of sound, vibrations gathering on the lips, escape of sound from the lips), you are naturally making more demands on your breathing. You have begun, in effect, to use longer sentences. They are primitive sentences, but the earlier the exercise "huh-hummmmmuh" or "βμμμμ" can be regarded as a sentence with an impulse to communicate and with three words in it, the faster thought/speech impulses in the brain can be conditioned to spontaneous integration with breath/sound responses in the body. Be sure, therefore, in dealing with longer "sentences", however primitive, to sustain the *thought*, which will automatically make the breath last. You need never try to sustain the *breath* as such; it will serve the sustained thought.

It is very important never to continue the sound until you run out of breath. Let each set of sounds have an easy, rhythmic pattern that stimulates the breath but does not punish it. The breath serves the thought and each thought has an intrinsic length. Each new thought has a new breath: Short thoughts have short breaths, medium thoughts have medium breaths and long thoughts have long breaths, but seldom does an organic thought drive the breath through to the last gasp. No purpose whatsoever is served by learning to sustain a breath over a longer and longer span of time; all that happens is that the natural elasticity of the breathing muscles is impaired, and capacity is reduced because the effort involved creates tension and tension contracts. Everyone has a natural breathing capacity which, when free of inhibitory tension, is fully capable of serving the individual emotional and imaginative capacity. The assumption here is that work on the voice is in the interest of the human truth it expresses. If you want to develop the voice as a musical instrument you can have a different attitude to the breath and manipulate it at will.

I shall use the suggestion "sigh out on a hum," "sigh the sound into your head," and so on, quite regularly in the early exercises. This is to condition a combined muscular and emotional release at the beginning of every sound. The responsibility for *sustaining* the breath throughout a sentence is thus relegated to mental activity.

There is basic mental conditioning contained in the treatment of "huh-hummmmmuh" as a sentence with a beginning, a middle and an end. The touch of sound, "huh huh," is the beginning; the gathering of vibrations on the lips, "mmmmmm," is the middle; the escape of vibrations from the lips, "uh," is the end. Through the application of awareness, your mind should be contained in each of the "words" that make up this sentence, and this programs the unification of thought and sound. When you "sigh with relief" through each sentence, you involve yourself on a feeling level as well as a mental and physiological one. A sigh of relief is a very easy feeling to induce, and if you commit yourself to that feeling as an integral component of these early exercises, you will be practicing the synthesis of feeling, thought, body and voice in simple ways which will make it that much easier to deal with a free attack on "Once more into the breach, dear friends . . ." or "Brave warriors, Clifford and Northumberland, come, make him stand upon this molehill here . . ." when the occasion arises.

Remembering that no vibrations can exist freely unless the breath is free, let us return to the vibrations that amplify sound, with an exploration of what happens when the whole head and neck area starts to relax. Tension, to a greater or lesser degree, is common in the back of the neck, the jaw and throat. As long as such tension exists in such a vital part of the vocal channel, vibrations are trapped in contracted muscles. The job will be to release those vibrations by undoing the tension. The aim in the following exercises will be to get rid of your head. Physiologically you will be rolling your head around in a loose circle; psychologically you will be transferring yourself from your head to your middle, so that the controlling center is not in the shopping list part of the brain, but deep inside the body.

STEP 5 ■ *Stand easily, feet just apart, spine long, stomach muscles relaxed.*

Focus on the back of the neck and picture the top seven vertebrae of the spine that comprise the neck.

Let the whole neck drop forward, suddenly and heavily.

Now roll the neck (the top seven vertebrae) to the right, until the head hangs over the right shoulder.

Register the pull on the tendons in the left side of the neck as the head drops heavily in one direction and the left shoulder in the opposite direction.

Let the neck fall backwards allowing the head to drop heavily off the end, jaw relaxed, mouth dropped open, throat stretched.

From there, let the neck roll over to the left shoulder.

Register the stretching tendons in the right side of the neck as the head drops heavily away from the right shoulder.
Then let the weight of the head and neck fall heavily forward.

You have thus rolled the head in a wide circle from right to left. You roll the neck, and the head goes with it.

■ *Roll the neck (and head) loosely from right to left, and then from left to right, on to the shoulder (feel the stretch in the opposite tendons), back (let the mouth and throat drop open), up on to the shoulder (feel the stretch), forward (heavy).*
Let the neck be active and the head passive.

If you roll the head you will tend to twist the neck and involve only the top three or four vertebrae. The neck should be moving from the big bone that sits at the bottom of the neck and the top of the body-spine. You can check to see whether you are involving the neck as fully as possible by noticing where your face is in relation to your shoulder as you roll over the side. You should, if you are really releasing the neck from its base, be looking straight ahead as you go over the shoulder. If your head is the activator, you will tend to be looking at the shoulder, or at the floor as you go over the sides. Your ear lobe should be directly above the shoulder in the side position, another checkpoint.

■ *Roll the head and neck slowly, heavily, from right to left several times.*
Roll it from left to right several times.
Then roll it a little faster, allowing a momentum to take over.

Remember that the objective in rolling the head and neck is to relax the muscles at the back of the neck, and begin to release the throat, tongue, larynx and jaw; that is, to free the channel through which sound travels.

STEP 6   ■ *Leave the head dropped back for a moment.*
Focus your mind firmly on the back of the neck and straighten up through the neck vertebrae until the neck is in alignment with the rest of the spine and the head is balanced easily on the top vertebra.

STEP 7   ■ *Tune into the breathing center and sigh a hum from there into your head.*
        Mmmmmmmmmmmmmmmmmmm (on your lips).
        (Sigh of relief underneath.)

Immediately you feel the vibrations on your lips.

Drop your head and neck forward and roll them round in a loose circle as explored in Step 5.

Relax in your middle and let the breath drop back in. Sigh a hum into your head.

Drop your head forward and roll it round the other way.

Relax for the new breath.

Hum again (on pitch) and roll in the other direction.

■ *Don't go too long on each breath. Let the breath have its own life without being pushed till you are empty.*

■ *Find a new pitch for each new head roll, going up three or four notes, then down three or four notes.*

Despite the fact that your lips are now closed to form a hum, let your throat and jaw relax open behind them as your head drops backwards. The lips are elastic enough to cover the gap, and the effect is similar to stifling a yawn in polite company, keeping the lips together, but yawning somewhere in the recesses of the throat.

STEP 8　■ *Bring your neck up into alignment with the rest of the spine.*

■ *Sigh a hum on pitch into your head and feel with your fingers all the different places that are vibrating with sound.*

■ *Touch your lips — cheeks — nose — forehead — top of the skull — back of your neck — throat — chest.*

■ *Take enough time to explore fully, both with your fingertips and your awareness, how the vibrations feel in the different places.*

You will notice that the vibrations are much stronger in some places than in others, but don't be prejudiced in favor of the strong ones. Get to know the quality of the lighter, weaker vibrations as well as the rich, strong ones.

With the added awareness of all the places you have explored tactilely,

■ *Once more, roll your head and neck on a hum. Sigh the hum out.*
　Mmmmmmmmmmmmmmm

Feel the vibration in your lips — your face — your skull — your throat — your chest.

Roll your head in the other direction humming on a new pitch. Notice the emphasis of vibration shift according to whether your head is dropped forward or backward.

Imagine the vibrations are like ball-bearings inside a round box, shifting and rolling as the box rolls.

STEP 9   ■ *Repeat the "huh-hummmmmuhs" as practiced in Step 3 with the physical awareness of all the vibrations that you felt in the head now pouring into your speaking voice. Indulge the feeling of sound and realize that it is your voice.*

Keep reminding yourself that you are not just doing vocal exercises; you are aiming to *free your natural speaking voice.* Beyond that, the aim is to *free yourself* through your voice. Although I can give clues as to how to achieve those aims physiologically, only you know what these might mean for you as an individual. After each exercise find a perfectly simple, personal thing to say, and say it out loud, with an awareness of what you have just been doing "technically." For instance:

■ *Sigh with relief through the touch of sound "huh-huh."*
Wallow in vibration on "mmmmmmmm." Let the vibrations escape into the air on "uh."
Let the breath replace and then:
Sigh out "that feels good" with the same physical awareness that you had on "huh-hummmmmmmuh."
Or sigh out "I wish I knew what I was doing" or "I'm hungry and I want my dinner" or anything that expresses the feeling you have at this moment.

■ *Relax, shake yourself, move about, jump up and down, stop concentrating.*

You have loosened the lips in order to free vibrations from them; you have loosened your head and neck in order to free vibrations from them; in Step 10 you will be loosening the whole body to free more vibrations from an even larger area. This is a progression of exercises for releasing vibrations that can amplify basic sound which moves logically from small to large.

STEP 10   ■ *Stand easily — spine long — head floating up off the topmost vertebra.*
Relax the stomach muscles so that the natural rhythm of breathing takes over.
Choose an easy, mid-register pitch and sigh a hum on to your lips.

■ *Now let your head and neck drop heavily forward.*
Give in to the weight and drop down through the spine.

Vibrations that amplify the initial sound   49

Hang your head downward.

Relax inside and let the breath replace.

Make sure your neck is relaxed, your knees bent, so that you are comfortably balanced.

Hum again hanging upside down and notice how the vibrations behave in this position.

Hum again as you hang there and gently shake your body loose.

Where do the vibrations predominate?

Let the breath replace.

■ *Hum again (on another note) and build up your spine to a standing position as you hum.*

Register the shifting emphasis of the vibrations.

Where do they predominate when you are upside down?

Where do they arrive when you are upright again?

■ Do not take too long building up the spine; if the breath does not last easily, let a new breath in. If you build slowly, you should allow two or three breaths; if you go faster, you can do it on one. Do not stay hanging upside down for too long or you will become unnecessarily dizzy. Take it easy; explore the sensations.

■ *Repeat the process (dropping down the spine on a hum, and building up again) on different pitches.*

■ *Then drop down the spine on a hum.*

Let an easy breath come in.

Build up on a hum quite quickly and at the top let your mouth drop open so that the sound can escape.

Imagine that in the course of dropping down the spine (which was established in Chapter 3 as a relaxation exercise for the whole body) you are freeing vibrations from the whole torso. Imagine that when you reach the upright position again, all those free, loose vibrations are thriving inside the body but are trapped by your lips and longing to be free of you. When you open your lips you allow all the vibrations that were imprisoned inside you to escape into the air.

■ *Play with the whole process again, getting to know the vibrations and what they feel like, as though they had a life of their own which you can encourage or diminish.*

■ *Personalize the vibrations so that you may be pleasurably involved with them, thus producing a feeling that can underlie the exercise. From that, you can practice freeing your feelings simultaneously with the sound.*

The introduction of the word *feelings* into a supposedly technical exercise for vibrations leads me to underline what I hope is becoming obvious, namely a technique which uses the imagination to unify in one place within the body, mind, feeling, breath and sound. It is an economical way of looking at the process of communicating, for the time being, and avoids the necessity of coordinating skill.

I will now arrange a short workout to cover the exercises explored up to this point. This will be a suggested pattern of work combining the movements and sounds that must be repeated often if they are to re-program the communicative channels, with accompanying admonitions as to where the attention should focus at any particular moment.

Intermission: Workout for relaxation, the spine, the head, breathing, touch of sound, humming

■ Lie on your back on the floor.

Choose, from your memory, a place which gives you a particularly good sense of peace, tranquility and relaxation: lying on a beach, in a green meadow in the sun, on a boat, but not your bed. Imagine you are lying in that place and can give your limbs up and let your muscles relax. It helps to have the sun in your picture, or a warm fire.

■ Take time to let your mind move slowly through your body from the toes to the top of the head undoing any tiny pockets of tension that you find in the course of the journey. If you do this in the context of a clearly visualized and remembered place that you like, the process of specific relaxation will probably be accompanied by feelings of pleasure.

Allow these feelings to color as much of the subsequent work as possible.

■ Turn your attention to the tiny involuntary rise and fall of natural, relaxed breathing deep in the center of your body. Let your lips fall apart and feel the outgoing breath escape over the front of your mouth making a small "fff" as it leaves your body. Wait for the breath to replace in its own time.

■ Continue your awareness of the natural breathing rhythm until it seems genuinely to have found its own pace and place deep inside.

■ Then send an impulse for sound down to the center of the diaphragm. Let the breath turn to sound.

Huh-huh

*Repeat the sound on each outgoing breath in the rhythm of your
natural breathing.*

Huh-huh ∅ huh-huh ∅ huh-huh ∅

■ *Alternate "huh-huh" and "fff" to see how close you can stay to
the sensation of just breathing when you add sound.*

■ *Make sure the "huh-huh" is a pure sound and the "fff" is a pure
breath.* It sometimes helps to think of sound as black, breath as white,
and a breathy, mixed sound as gray. All that is needed to achieve a
"black" sound while releasing the breath is a really clear thought. If
your sounds are "gray" you are probably concentrating too much on
relaxation for its own sake and not enough on what you want to do
through that relaxation.

■ *Now introduce the thought of descending pitches. Start on a
comfortable mid-register note and gradually drop down, if possible,
semitone by semitone, or tone by tone.*

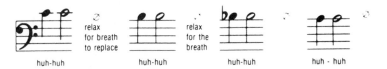

and so on, until the sound is so low and loose that it almost gargles.

■ *See how low you can go without pushing down. Relax deeper and
deeper inside your body for the deeper sounds; as soon as you feel
you have to strain at all, start moving up in pitch again. Stay within
the natural breathing rhythm.*

■ *Speak the sound again "huh-huh."*

■ *Then slowly begin to get up from the floor, economically, main-
taining as much relaxation as possible.*
Stand, feet just apart.
Yawn and stretch throughout your body.
Stretch up to the ceiling.
*Then let your wrists go, elbows, arms, head, top of the spine, give
in to the weight of the shoulders and head dragging on the spine,
until you drop, hanging head downward from the tailbone.*

■ *Sigh into your back, letting your diaphragm give in to gravity as
the breath releases.*
Build up your spine, vertebra by vertebra.
Head floats up on top.
Stomach muscles loose.
Knees free.

Spine long.

Breathe easily, giving in to the involuntary rhythm.

■ Small fff's.

Huh-huh.

Huh-hummmmuh.

Blow out through the lips without sound to loosen them.

Move all the face muscles around.

Blow out through the lips on sound ßμμμμmmmmmmuh.

Repeat on descending pitches.

ßß μμμμ = loosen the vibrations = blow out through lips
mmmmmmm = gather the vibrations = close the lips
uh = free the vibrations = open the lips

ßßμμμμμmmmmmmmmuh

ßßμμμmmmmuh

sigh it out from the center

Ø   relax for the breath to replace

ßßμμμmmmmuh

register vibrations all over the face

Ø   relax for the breath

ßßμμμmmmmmm
uh

Move your lips around on the hum
taste them

Ø

ßßßμμμμmmmuh

looser and looser lips

Ø

huh-hummmmuh

be aware of the touch of sound

Ø

huh-hummmmmuh

try to induce a sigh of relief
underneath it

Ø

huh-hummmmmuh

touch of sound
register the vibrations on the lips
let the sound go free

huh-hummmmmmuh

sigh it out more freely

■ *Now, speak it huh-hummmmmuh with the same physical
awarenesses as when you sang.*

*Relax for a new breath ⊘ and speak it again huh-hummmmmmuh
with conversational inflection.*

Ask a question through huh-hummmmmmuh.

*Notice whether, as soon as you think about "speaking," your focus
tends to move up into your face. Send the "question" impulse
clearly down to the feeling/breathing center, and let the question/
breath/vibration response flow up and out through the torso, throat
and mouth. Add surprise, urgency, doubt or amusement to the
question and the central connection will be pinpointed by the
feeling content.*

■ *Drop the head heavily forward, and then roll it loosely around in
a wide circle to relax the neck and throat muscles.*

Circle it in the other direction.

Hum on an easy pitch, as you roll your head.

*With a new note, a new breath impulse and a new hum, roll your
head in the other direction.*

*Repeat four or five hums on different pitches, with your head rolling
in alternating directions.*

Check that you are humming on a pure mmmmmmm.

Only the lips should be touching to form the hum. The tongue should
not be touching the roof of the mouth in the middle, the sides or the
back. The sound, originating in the center, should meet no impeding
surface until it meets the closed lips. Conversely, there should be
space behind the lips, clear down to the breathing center.

■ *Roll your head and hum a few more times to be aware of the above.*

Don't squeeze the breath out to the last drop; stop before getting tight
inside. Try to induce a sigh impulse under each new breath so that
the exercise does not become mechanical. Have the courage to let
your head really drop at the front and at the back. If you are saving it,
you are probably also tightening your jaw or throat or tongue.

■ Bring your head up to its balance point. Describe out loud how you feel, and what you feel — immediately, spontaneously, without censoring it. Release the feeling of how you feel into the sound.

■ Now let the hum start in your middle again and let your head drop forward. Let the weight of your head take you all the way down your spine until you are hanging head downwards.
Feel the vibrations dropping out through the top of your head.
Register whatever sensations occur.
Make sure your knees are slightly bent — weight in the middle of the feet — stomach muscles relaxed.
Let the breath replace ∅

In this position notice that the back can respond to the breathing need more freely than the front; take advantage of this awareness.

■ Hum again, and build your spine up again to standing, let your lips open at the top to allow the sound to escape.
∅ relax inside to let the breath replace, on a slightly higher pitch, repeat the exercise.
Drop down through the spine on a hum;
New breath at the bottom.
New hum.
Build up the spine.
Release the sound at the top letting the mouth
Drop easily open.

Let what is happening to your body affect the sound. There may be a wish to preserve the sound in a straight, unwavering line, but that is a false sense of control. Whatever the body does should affect the sound, so let the vibrations get moved around and shaken as your body drops down.

■ Alternate the humming-and-head-rolling, and the humming-and-dropping-down-through-the-spine on changing pitches. Begin to explore slightly higher notes in the context of this exercise.
Use your awarenesses in speaking again; huh-hummmmmuh.
Finally, forget everything you have done, and read or speak a poem, a speech, some dialogue from a play.

When you come back to a text, you should focus all your interest on the content and meaning of that text, and be prepared to judge whether your voice has been freed at all by the subjective criterion of your enjoyment of your work.

7: The channel for sound

Work on the voice must fluctuate constantly between freeing the breathing muscles which deal with the source of sound, and freeing throat, tongue and jaw muscles which constitute the channel through which the sound travels.

We have dealt, to a certain extent, with how to release the breath more fully, thereby providing essential support for sound. But there are many muscles on the journey which the voice makes through the body which wrongly consider their help vital to sound-making. As long as the muscles of the jaw, tongue and throat provide support for sound, the breath will remain lazy in the performance of its duties. It is important, but sometimes difficult, to become aware of such false support in order to remove it and focus the work where it belongs. Work on the channel is primarily negative; work on the source, positive. Negative and positive messages must be sent simultaneously: Relax the channel, stimulate the source. Gradually, as the source support becomes surer, the channel muscles can take a much needed rest and be available for their true functions.

Generally speaking, the jaw's true functions are: (a) to hold teeth and chew food, and (b) to widen the exit when some powerful emotional/vocal content needs to escape. The tongue's true function in speaking is to articulate vowels and consonants. The throat is composed of too many specific components to generalize in a way helpful to the simple picture attempted at this point, and will be discussed later.

Starting with the jaw, the first step is to break down the general picture of the head and neck. The skull is split into two large bony structures joined by a hinge. As both these structures have teeth, and as "head" and "skull" are too general, I shall call one the top jaw and the other the bottom jaw for the time being.

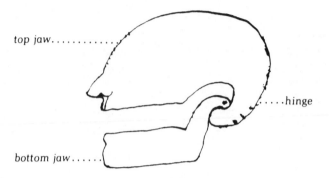

It is helpful to imagine the bottom jaw as being hooked on to the top jaw, rather like a false beard, right beside the ears. There is plenty of play in the hook mechanism, and the most effective space between the top and bottom jaws is found when the bottom jaw drops down and back. It is much more common to find that it is down and *forward* when the mouth is wide open, despite the fact that it has to be pushed to get there, making a very inelastic passageway which allows too slow a response to changing demands of communication.

jaw at rest   pushed down and forward: dropping down and back:
                       out of the hinge   still hooked in

It is natural for the bottom jaw to drop toward the back of the neck when the muscles in the hinge are fully relaxed. Yet tension in the jaw is so common that ligaments shorten, muscles contract, effort is needed to open the mouth and the effort can push the jawbone forward, forcing the hook out of the hinge almost far enough to dislocate the connection. It is rare for someone working on this area to react naturally to the idea of dropping the jaw. The idea is complicated by the knowledge that you drop your jaw to open your mouth, and "open your mouth wider" is the advice given by old-style elocutionists, high school singing teachers and even frustrated directors who can't hear a word the actor is saying. The unconscious image evoked by that admonition deals with the front of the face and yet the essential space needed is at the back of the mouth, not the front. Indeed trying to open wide in front can mean closing more at the back through sheer effort, thus defeating the main objective which is to give the voice more room.

The muscles joining the top jaw and the bottom jaw are complexly interwoven with those spreading through the face and the back of the neck. They go vertically, horizontally, diagonally, internally and externally. To get maximum response in this top part of the voice channel it helps to think of the bottom jaw dropping *and the top jaw lifting*, from as far back as possible. The top jaw action takes some of the burden off the bottom jaw as far as supplying space is concerned, diminishes the danger of pressing the tongue and larynx down, which can cause strain, and suggests spaces in the upper pharynx as added passages for sound.

This movement, up and back as well as down and back, when taken to an extreme, resembles instinctual reflex movement on an animal level in response to large emotional impulses of fear, anger, grief and joy. It can be easily seen in animals: a lion roaring, a dog attacking, a cat spitting in self-defense, and in the extremes of human emotion expressed in screaming or howling. The faces of people screaming with hysterical joy at a rock concert, or with hysterical fear and pain in battle, howling with mirth or howling with abandoned grief, move into similar muscle configuration whatever the specific emotional content.

In small children it is possible to see how the face reveals the nuance of intensifying feelings through a gradual opening of the face, but all too soon our guarded defenses against the onset of emotion largely condition our faces, throats and jaws against moving in those directions except in uncontrolled response to violent stimulus. It is almost impossible to express subtle and median feelings accurately and openly because the muscles have learned to behave in ways that disguise rather than reveal. To disguise the rictus of fear, the upper lip learns to stiffen bravely; to disguise the pleasure felt when one is complimented, the corners of the lips turn deprecatingly downward rather than up in a straight smile. To preserve the impression that one knows what is going on under any circumstances, the middle of the face immobilizes into impassiveness, quelling the ripples of anxiety, questioning, naive response that might give one away in a hostile world; sometimes a fixed smile of eternal appeasement imprints itself on the face of one who fears the strength of his and others' anger to kill and be killed.

One of the strongest and most universal muscular defense systems is in the jaw hinges. Clenching the teeth is a sure way to avoid opening the throat wide enough for a scream of fear to escape, so a bulging jaw muscle comes to represent bravery and strength. Many's the moment in the movies when the camera zooms in for a close-up of a set jaw and you know that battle will commence and the strong man will win. If the jaw muscle twitches, however, you must infer some conflicting emotion and inner struggle, even a little neurosis. "He bit back the anger that rose in him." "She bit her handkerchief to stifle her sobs." A piece of wood was put between the teeth of those about to be operated on before the days of anaesthetics, partly to prevent the patient's from biting their tongues, partly to keep them from screaming. We have been conditioned, subtly and not so subtly, to use the jaw more as an iron gate to be slammed shut against the onslaught of emotions than as a wide-flung portal through which imprisoned feelings can leap to freedom.

Few of us after the age of six or seven have the opportunity to scream daily, in joy or anger, or indeed to howl with laughter more than once or twice a week if lucky. Natural exercise for the jaw muscles is hard to come by, and, stretching so seldom, they lose their elasticity and length.

We do yawn, which is a help, but even that superbly therapeutic action is apt to be curtailed so as not to offend others. As you begin to work to free the jaw, the tongue and the throat, you will probably start to yawn a great deal. Indulge your yawns, encourage them, expand them: they stimulate circulation by increasing oxygen intake and they provide a spontaneous, natural stretch for important channel muscles more discreetly than by screaming regularly.

More than yawning is going to be necessary if the actor is to recondition the response of the jaw muscles to the impulse of feeling. Such reconditioning must happen because that which helps one to cope emotionally in terms of society can block one disastrously in terms of the theatre.

The first thing to do is to learn how to relax the jaw muscles, and to learn to recognize tension when it occurs in that somewhat hidden area.

Jaw awareness

Clench your teeth at the back and bite hard. Bite and relax several times and with your fingers feel the jaw muscles that are below the ear bunching and releasing.

Now yawn, and put your fingers in your ears as your jaw opens. You will feel the bony hinge movement both inside and just outside your ears. This is where to put your mind when you are asked to "let the jaw relax."

Jaw awareness exercises

STEP 1 ■ *Put the heel of your hands on the jaw hinge area either side of your face.*
Pressing quite heavily into the cheeks, smooth the bottom jaw down away from the top jaw until the mouth hangs loosely open.
Imagine that your bottom jaw has no muscles of its own and depends solely on your hand for movement. Put the back of your hand under the bottom jaw and with your hand lift the jaw up until the teeth touch lightly at the back of the mouth.

If your front teeth touch, you are pushing the jaw forward. It is relatively rare for the jaw to be set far enough forward for the front teeth to meet in a natural bite.

■ *Let it be the teeth that touch, not the lips.*
If you take your hand away the jaw must drop, given the imaginary circumstances of having no muscles of its own.

■ *Take your hand away.*
The jaw drops.

■ *Imagine little lead weights being attached to the back angle of the jawbone, below the ears, so that it drags down further.*

■ *With the back of the hand lift the jaw back up.*
Take the hand away.
With the hand lift the jaw up.
Repeat several times.

Your mind should be observing the result of this process in the jaw hinges. Without having to push the jaw down actively, the ligaments and muscles within the hinge mechanism should be getting gently stretched by the weight of the bone dragging at them. If you attempt this stretch by actively exercising the jaw you will impair the muscular elasticity and increase the muscular control.

STEP 2 ■ *With your neck long, head floating, put your thumbs under your jawbone and your fingers on top of it so that you have a firm grip on the jawbone on either side of the chin. Your hands are again the muscles for the bottom jaw.*
Start with the teeth closed lightly.

Throughout this exercise the actual jaw muscles are acted upon; they do not perform the movements.

- *Without moving the bottom jaw at all, lift the top jaw up and off the bottom jaw until the mouth is open.*

Using the hands, lift the bottom jaw up to meet the top jaw so that the teeth touch at the back.

Without moving the bottom jaw again lift the top jaw up and off the bottom jaw until the mouth is open.

Once more, with the hands, lift the bottom jaw up to the top jaw.

At this point, if you have managed to find out how to move your top jaw, your head should be as far back as it can go.

- *With your hands, bring your bottom jaw down.*

Your head will now be back, your mouth wide open and your jaw still in the grip of your hands.

- *Keep your bottom jaw where it is: Bring your top jaw up and over onto the bottom jaw.*

Question: Where are the muscles that move the top jaw? Try the exercise again and try to find out through your own observation before going on. This whole exercise is more mental than physical because it asks the mind to reroute its messages and relabel the destinations of those messages. It cannot, therefore, perform mechanically.

Having redone the preceding top jaw, bottom jaw exercise steps, perhaps you have found that the muscles moving the top jaw are in the back of the neck.

- *Repeat the whole process, clearly sending the messages first to the hands, then to the back of the neck.*

To the hands.

To the back of the neck.

And so on.

As the back of the neck takes on more responsibility for supporting the top jaw (the skull), the actual jaw muscles will be able to release more.

STEP 3 ■ *Think of lengthening the back of the neck to provide a strong support for the whole head.*

Take hold of the jaw with both hands, and gently swing it up and down, being aware that you are loosening the jaw muscles inside the hinge.

Don't waste time moving it from side to side; we do not use that movement in speaking, and it is too forceful and dislocatory to be helpful in relaxing. Don't move the jaw up and down with its own muscles during this exercise; you will only make them more efficient in controlling and defending your communication.

The tongue

The next area for work in the channel for sound is the tongue. The tongue is all flesh and muscle from the tip to the roots. The roots are attached by means of the hyoid bone to the larynx. If you examine your tongue both with the help of a mirror and with your mind's eye, you will perhaps realize that, although the tip is relatively familiar to you, there is a large area inside the mouth going down into your throat that you do not know much about and that seems to have a life of its own. Watch your tongue for a minute or two, with your mouth wide enough open for you to see right through to the back where it thickens. Observe whether it moves involuntarily, whether it is humped up in the middle or hollowed, whether it lies thick and relaxed with the tip touching the lower teeth, or thin and retracted. Within the thickness of the tongue lie muscles which are highly sensitive to the psychological condition. Nobody says, "I am so nervous my tongue's gone tight inside my mouth," though one might say in similar circumstances "my stomach's gone tight" or neck or shoulders. Yet any nervous tension, or habitual difficulty in communication, creates contractions in the tongue that pull it back, flatten it or bunch it up in the throat. Such contractions change the shape of the throat-mouth cavity, distorting the resonating response and the subsequent vocal quality. Since the tongue is joined to the larynx, the state of one area must affect the other. Either tension in the tongue spreads to the larynx affecting the free play of the vocal folds, or tension beginning in the larynx spreads to the tongue affecting articulation. Tension in the larynx also implies tension in the diaphragm and vice-versa.

For working purposes it is enough to regard the tongue as one of the compensating "helpful" muscles that assumes responsibility for sound when the breath is not free. If it is persuaded to take a rest the breath may start to take on its true function again, but the only argument for transferring all the support the voice needs to the breath is expressivity and a sensitive pickup of emotion. The tongue can support sound strongly without necessarily contributing to vocal strain. A "chest" voice, belted out in a high register, is largely dependent on muscular support from the back of the tongue; and some fascinating personality voices develop by virtue of a gradual takeover by the tongue muscles producing gravelly or hoarse two-note tones. But the tongue has no function in the natural formation of sound, and all the notes throughout the range of the voice can be produced without any tightening in the back of the tongue. For emotion to be expressed freely through the voice, the tongue must be relaxed.

Awareness of the tongue is developed initially by learning to stretch it fully and relax it consciously. You cannot stretch the tongue adequately by sticking it straight out of the mouth, as it is attached to the floor of the mouth in such a way that only a small section is affected. In order to stretch the tongue right down to its roots follow the exercises described next.

STEP 1   ■ *Place the tip of the tongue down behind the bottom teeth.*
Tongue stretching   *Think into the middle of the tongue and roll it forward and out of the mouth like a big wave breaking over the bottom teeth, until you feel it stretched from tip to roots.*

■ *Then let it relax back on the floor of the mouth, the tip still touching the bottom teeth.*

The active muscles should be in the middle of the tongue. As they roll forward they pull the back of the tongue up and out of the throat.

■ *Repeat the stretching/relaxing movements several times and observe the following points, applying them where necessary:*

If you press too hard into the bottom teeth you will push the jaw forward, creating tension in the jaw hinge and robbing the tongue of a full stretch. Try to let the jaw drop down and back. Think of lifting the top jaw up to create space in the upper part of the mouth channel through which the tongue can move freely.

Make sure that the upper lip and teeth lift well away from the tongue, and that the throat releases wide behind the tongue so that you are creating large spaces as the tongue stretches. At first the throat has a tendency to close during this exercise; to check whether this is happening, hold your nose and see if you can breathe. If you are breathing through your mouth while stretching the tongue, your throat is open.

Once the jaws are open to let the tongue out, leave them open. After the first stretch the only movement should be in the tongue;

the jaws remain wide. If you smile slightly during the exercise you will find the upper jaw lift is easier and the tongue movements freer.

Keep the tip of the tongue attached to the back of the bottom teeth both while rolling the tongue forward and when it relaxes back into the mouth. Use a mirror to see whether what you *feel* happening is actually happening. Your physical awareness is not yet to be trusted to feed you accurate information.

In the course of the exercise, whenever the tongue relaxes flat you should be able to see clear through to the back of your throat, but be sure it *relaxes* flat, don't pull it down.

There are so many individual patterns of tension possible in the tongue, the lips and the jaw that it is impossible to cover here all the things you may find happening in your mouth. A common difficulty is in isolating the tongue from the jaw and from the top lip which sometimes wants to come down to meet the tongue as it comes forward. Both must be encouraged to stay out of the exercise, which is for the benefit of the tongue. Another common problem is to be able to *relax* the tongue back after the stretch. If there is habitual contraction in the tongue muscles then the stretching, rolling forward movement is in direct opposition to the habitual state and it may take some persuasion to reverse the tendency to *pull* the tongue back.

STEP 2
Tongue loosening

■ *Let the tongue lie relaxed in the floor of the mouth with the tip lightly touching the back of the bottom teeth (this is the "home" position for a relaxed tongue).*

Gently move the middle of the tongue forward and back in a small-scale version of the previous exercise. This time the jaw remains relaxed with the teeth not more than 3/4" apart.

The tongue moves inside the mouth, barely going beyond the front teeth.

■ *Now gradually speed up the forward, back, forward, back movements of the middle-tongue until you feel you are lightly shaking the tongue loose throughout its length. You are loosening the tongue, not exercising it, no longer stretching it.*

The next objective will be to use your consciousness of tongue-loosening to see whether it can stay loose when sound is added.

The exercise will be to release sound from the breathing center, loosening the tongue at the same time, thereby proving that the tongue has no function in the basic sound-making process.

STEP 3
Loosening the
tongue with sound

■ *Sigh sound out from your breathing center (a sustained "huh") on pitch.*

 hu-u-u-u-uh

Picture a solid stream of vibrations flowing from your middle up and out through your mouth; then loosen your tongue, rolling it gently forward and back as the sound streams out over it.

Try to do this exercise with 100% physical awareness. Try not to be distracted by what your ear tells you. For the moment explore the physical sensations arrived at by the application of clear mental pictures and clear physical instructions. Remember that if you had no tongue the sound could flow with complete freedom through a wide, unblocked channel. Imagine the ease with which you could do voice exercises if the tongue were detachable and could be removed at the beginning of a vocal workout; only when you came to articulation would you have to put it back in. Your aim in the following exercises should be to get rid of the tongue as nearly as possible and to observe what happens to the sound as a result.

■ *Practice Step 3 applying the following points of awareness:*
Feed a real impulse for a sigh of relief into your feeling/breathing center and free it out into the sound.

 hu-u-u-u-uh

Loosen the middle-tongue, rolling it forward and back as the sound sighs through your mouth:

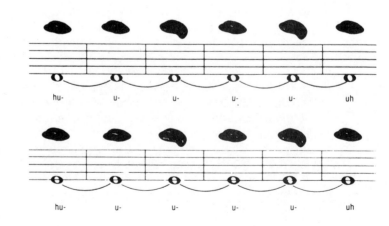

and so on, continuing up the register as far as you can go comfortably without pushing.

Observe, meanwhile, that (1) the jaw stays loose, (2) the stomach relaxes for each ingoing breath, (3) you sigh more fully as you go higher, (4) the sound sighs forward on a horizontal line out of the mouth and into the air rather than dropping onto the tongue and being pulled back into the throat (see illustrations).

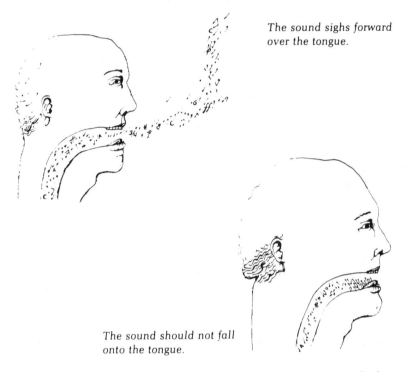

The sound sighs forward over the tongue.

The sound should not fall onto the tongue.

■ Now expand your awareness to take in the changing sounds that occur as your tongue moves. The vibrations no longer arrive in a straight "hu-uh-uh-uh" but are molded by the tongue movements into new shapes. Notice what sound is happening when the tongue rolls forward, and when the tongue relaxes. You will perhaps discover that as the tongue rolls forward the sound resembles a loose Y. So that what is happening is this:

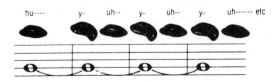

■ *Repeat the exercise carrying out the physical steps that result in that sound.*

This is a very important point. The physical awareness is the working area; you can expand that awareness to take in the resultant sound aurally but if you merely repeat the sound you heard, if you merely say "hu-yuh-yuh," you achieve the opposite to the desired result, because you are using the tongue as an articulator and exercising its muscular ability. The desired result of these exercises is to remove the tongue from the basic sound-making process. This may seem a fine distinction, but it is precisely the refined mental exercise involved in encompassing that distinction which helps to reprogram the route of the communicating impulse from brain to diaphragm and to recondition the use of the voice causally.

STEP 4
Reprogramming
the impulse route

■ *Repeat Step 3 (tongue loosening with sound) applying the following pictures:*
Visualize the stream of vibrations springing from their source in the breathing center and flowing out through the mouth above the tongue which is relaxing, loosening, getting out of the way underneath the sound.

The stream of vibrations is active/positive energy. The tongue loosening is passive/negative energy.

■ *Repeat the whole process on ascending pitches. As soon as it becomes difficult to keep the tongue loose, come down again noticing the increased relaxation as you descend. Use your awareness of this relaxation for Step 5.*

STEP 5

■ *Let the tongue lie relaxed on the floor of the mouth, tip touching the back of the bottom teeth:*
Touching sound on center, speak "huh-huh"

⊘ "huh-hummmuh

⊘ *Buuuu*mmmmuh

⊘

Roll your head on a hum; repeat two or three times in alternating directions.

Drop down the spine on a hum ⊘ *come up and release the sound at the top; repeat two or three times on ascending and descending pitches.*

Questions: Do you notice any change in the feeling of the vibrations from the last time you did this exercise?
How does your mouth feel?

68   The freeing process

Has your breathing altered in any way? Or your perception of it? How do you feel? What do you feel?

Step 6 will use basically the same tongue movements as before but with a more specific aim and thinking process. The premise on which the next exercise is based is that if the tongue is free, the sound will be freed forward and will arrive unimpeded in the front of the mouth. The aim is to encourage this possibility, and the specific thought process should emphasize the forward part of the tongue roll, as though the tongue rolled the sound forward into the teeth.

STEP 6   ■ *Roll the middle-tongue forward (tip of the tongue down behind the bottom teeth) as described in Step 2 for tongue loosening, and leave it in the forward position.*

Notice that in this position there is a very narrow space left between the surface of the tongue and the upper gum ridge, and release sound from the breathing center through that space. The vibrations, molded by the narrow space, will naturally form a "heee" sound.

■ *Play with the tongue position until you feel the vibrations against the top teeth. Whisper "hee" aiming the breath over the tongue into the top teeth; then voice it.*

■ *Let the tongue relax flat on the floor of the mouth. The space between the surface of the tongue and the upper gum ridge is now larger, and the only sound that can happen without altering the space is "huh."*

Play with the two tongue positions and repeat the forward rolled vibrations "hee-hee-hee," and then the tongue-relaxed vibrations "huh-huh-huh."

■ *Going from "hee-hee-hee" (tongue rolled forward) to "huh-huh-huh" (tongue flat), use a mental image of the tongue actually rolling the vibrations forward into the teeth on the "hee"; then, as the tongue drops back into the mouth, picture the vibrations moving on forward and out of the mouth on the "huh's."*

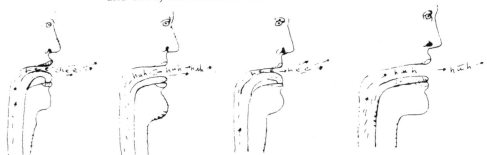

- Let the breath drop in between each set of sounds. Do not lose connection with the central starting point.

- Practice on ascending and descending pitches.

- Now on one long breath, alternate the "hee" and "huh" three times. Sigh out the "hee" rolling the tongue forward, and without a new breath drop the tongue flat letting the sound change to "huh": Repeat twice more.

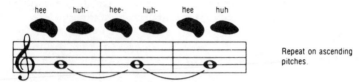

Repeat on ascending pitches.

- Do the same thing taking out the connecting "h's."

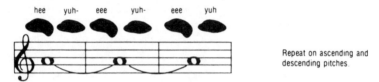

Repeat on ascending and descending pitches.

Add to the above a consciously repeated impulse for a sigh of relief to spark the new breath for each new pitch.

You will no doubt discover that Step 6 is very similar to Step 3. What has changed is the mental use of the tongue loosening. The mind is now making a greater demand in that it must know that the sound predominates in the front of the mouth as the tongue frees up and out of the throat. This more specific thinking process is not possible until the basic tongue relaxation has been explored, and awareness of the area sharpened.

Notice that I have begun to suggest that you go higher in pitch as you exercise. Having established some consciousness of relaxation you can now feed in greater demands and use your consciousness to abolish unnecessary efforts in meeting those demands.

As you go higher observe whether the tongue wants to behave differently from its behavior on the lower, easier notes. Does it roll forward as loosely and simply?

Is it still soft underneath the jaw? (Put a finger in the soft place between the jawbones on the underside of the mouth: There you can feel the condition of the tongue muscles, which should always be soft, even when moving.) Is the tongue falling flat on to the floor of the mouth on the second part of the movement, or is it starting to pull back?

Do not rely on your subjective awareness of these points; it is not yet to be trusted. Use a mirror to check for any tiny changes in the behavior of the tongue when dealing with higher and lower notes in the range. The work will aim to arrive at the point where there is no difference whatsoever in the reaction of the tongue to intensifying vocal demand, whether it is higher pitch, larger emotion or greater volume. All these belong within the precinct of breath and resonance. The tongue must be left free to cope with articulation: The increasing and decreasing intensity and pace with which thoughts demand to be articulated in words.

As you continue to practice Step 6 with the aim of gradually increasing your range upward, be aware of what is happening in the breathing center whenever the tongue begins to harden, contract, retract, become tense. You will find that when the tongue tenses you are also tense in the breathing area, or that nothing appears to be happening there at all.

Your tongue tightens to provide support in compensation for weak, lazy, dead breathing. In order to leave the tongue free as you go higher in your range all you need think of doing is to sigh from *deeper down* with more and more relief. This will provide the essential breath, and, if you can honestly induce a real feeling of relief at the beginning of each sound, you will release your mind from its habitual reaction to greater demand which is either "I can't" or "If I try harder, if I push, if I am determined and really work perhaps to the point of suffering a bit, I'll make it." Don't suffer, don't try, don't work, just sigh with relief. This attitude can initiate a blueprint of psycho-physical response leading to a mutually beneficial interdependence of a free voice and free emotions.

The soft palate

We took the via negativa in working on the jaw and the tongue: Remove tension in order to allow something new to happen. For the next part of the channel for sound we will seem to be working more positively and directly to limber up certain muscles. In fact, the via negativa still holds true, because the aim will be to remove a condition of desuetude in the soft palate musculature, restoring a natural ability to respond on the involuntary level which will give full functioning back to some unused resonating channels.

The palate is hard and bony in front (the upper gum ridge), hard and domed in the middle (the roof of the mouth) and soft and fleshy at the very back (the soft palate). From the middle of the soft palate the uvula hangs down above the back of the tongue, a small, fleshy, vestigial appendage. In some people the uvula is rather long and in some it has virtually disappeared. A long uvula can contribute to a somewhat hoarse or guttural tone; sometimes it prevents a clear use of the upper register. In such cases, regular and conscientious exercise of the soft palate will result in a shorter uvula and a clear passageway.

On either side of the uvula the soft palate is all flesh and muscle. It can be regarded for working purposes in two ways: As the doorway from the throat into the mouth, and also as the trapdoor up into the middle and upper resonators.

Without regular, extended vocal exercise, the soft palate tends to become lazy or stiff. If it is lazy it hangs down like a heavy curtain at the back of the mouth absorbing and muffling vibrations. In this condition it is hard for the sound to travel clearly through the mouth cavity. Some of it will stop at the doorway and some will be rerouted through the nose. Nasality nearly always results from a lazy, dead, soft palate. If the soft palate is stiff the voice will be monotonous because one of the functions of the soft palate is to respond to changing pitches with tiny changes in muscle tone which almost invisibly lift and lower it as the pitch goes up or down. When you speak, pitch is constantly changing in response to thought inflection (in a free voice) so the freedom of the soft palate to respond on an involuntary level is essential to accurately nuanced communication. Such movement in the soft palate is very subtle in speaking, but it can be easily seen to lift in response to the thought of a sung high note. Open your mouth wide and look in a mirror at the soft palate. Think a high note and you should immediately see the soft palate lift in an involuntary response to the thought.

I cannot over-emphasize that these movements occur naturally on the involuntary level of the nervous system. Their malfunctioning is an almost inevitable outcome of human conditioning. Any work we do is to restore the possibility of the involuntary connection. If, having observed that the soft palate lifts in response to the thought of a high note, you proceed to lift the soft palate whenever you want to sing a high note, you defeat the aim of a free, natural voice. The conscious mind cannot operate those muscles with enough subtlety to preserve the expressive integrity of the natural voice. It can, however, tone up and tune up the muscles so that they respond with more agility to the involuntary demands. We shall begin to work on the soft palate in its capacity as the doorway from the throat into the mouth. As the muscles tone up, vibrations will be released more easily into the mask and head resonators; hence its second name of "trapdoor" upward.

STEP 1 ■ *Establish where the soft palate is by looking at it in a mirror with light shining directly into a wide open mouth.*

Put the mirror down and relax your mouth without closing it.

Very gently whisper (just breath, no voice at all) the syllable "kaa."

Focus into the place where the "K" is formed and observe minutely what happens for that little noise to occur, using your physical awareness and your mind's eye.

You should find that the back of the tongue rises to touch the hard palate just in front of the soft palate, breath is momentarily trapped behind the soft palate, then is released with a sharp pop as the two surfaces spring apart. For the following exercises, think of the "K" being formed between the back of the tongue and the actual soft palate (a little further back than the K used in speaking).

Think a definite "aaah" after the "K," not "uh" or "aw," so that the tongue and the soft palate will be quite far apart and the breath will neither gargle over the uvula nor scrape downward into the throat.

■ *Again whisper a clear, clean "kaa" being aware of the impact of soft palate and back of tongue.*

Then whisper "kaa" on an incoming breath.

Out again normally on "kaa," then whisper "kaa" as the breath goes in.

In the rhythm of ordinary breathing, whisper "kaa" as you breathe in and as you breathe out.

(On the incoming breath the "K" will happen as the back of the tongue and the soft palate are blown apart from in front by the breath trying to get in. On the outgoing breath it will happen as they are blown apart from behind by the breath trying to get out.)

■ *As you continue breathing in and out on whispered "kaa's" be aware of the different temperature of breath on the incoming and outgoing: Cool, coming in; warm, going out.*

Register which surfaces of the mouth are hit by the cool air.

Check that the front of the tongue stays relaxed, tip touching the back of the bottom teeth.

Put your hand on your breathing area to feel a springy central response to the springy channel.

■ *Focus clearly into the sensation of cool air hitting the soft palate as it rises off the whispered ingoing "kaa."*

Begin to give the cool air more space in the soft palate area.

When you whisper "kaa" on the outgoing breath, think of giving the warm breath as much space in the soft palate as the cool air had.

You are now working on the flexibility of the soft palate by asking it to respond to sensory stimuli. At the same time you are training your mind to be able to connect with an esoteric set of muscles normally not under conscious control. This you can do only through a sharpened awareness.

■ *Now yawn wide and examine the behavior of the soft palate in the mirror as you yawn. It will spontaneously lift and stretch much further than you can consciously lift and stretch it, but if you focus your attention into the actual yawn muscles you can use that awareness to extend your conscious work on the soft palate.*

Yawning is so pleasurable that it is easy to get lost in the overall sensation, but you can make good use of a yawn, so it is worth harnessing your attention to the specifics that make up the whole, and even reprogramming the yawn a little to spread its benefits further.

A short digression into the yawn

Do you yawn vertically or horizontally?

Most people favor the vertical yawn and most of the stretching occurs in a downward direction. The face pulls down and the jaw pushes down. If you begin to think more horizontally as you yawn you can reprogram it so that you in fact arrive at a completely circular opening, stretching both vertically and horizontally. You will find much more emphasis on a huge stretch in the soft palate, the throat and the middle of the face. You should be able to see all your teeth exposed, the soft palate stretched high and wide and have a clear view through to the very back wall of the throat.

If you have managed in the course of this exploration to induce several genuine yawns you will be in a good, healthy state to con-

the vertical yawn

the horizontal yawn

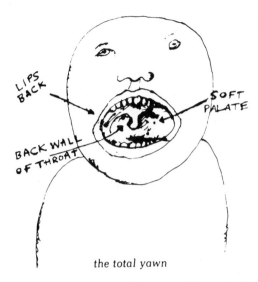

LIPS BACK

SOFT PALATE

BACK WALL OF THROAT

the total yawn

tinue. Your eyes and nose will run and so will your saliva, your breathing apparatus has been stimulated and you have been in perfect touch with involuntary processes while being aware of them.

STEP 2   ■ *Look in a mirror and repeat the exercise in Step 1.*

Now use your awareness of the yawn muscles to induce exactly the same stretch as you had when you yawned as you breathe in on the whispered "kaa." (It is important that you yawn horizontally or you may tend to gag.)

■ *Now use your awareness to lift the soft palate into the yawn stretch on the outgoing "kaa."*

Breathe in and out on a whispered "kaa," lifting and stretching the soft palate to its fullest, yawning extent each time.

Repeat two or three times, then rest, swallow, and moisten the throat which will have become rather dry.

As your throat becomes more accustomed to the cold air traveling through it you will be less bothered by dryness or the coughing that sometimes happen in the beginning. Don't be put off by the unfamiliar feeling of so much cold air going into your throat. It will not harm you, and if you avoid the process you may be perpetuating a habitual unwillingness to open the throat, which, though a vulnerable area, can suffer badly from an exaggerated instinct to protect it.

■ *Practice the exercise again with the following observations:*

The movements should be springy and the stretch should be elastic. Do not hold the stretch position.

The breath should feel and sound light and transparent.

Be careful not to drag the breath in. It should feel as though it is traveling through the spaces of the throat, not scraping over the walls.

Gradually speed up the process, so that the exercise becomes staccato, fast, light and elastic with a good stretch still experienced.

Read through the following steps so that when you do the exercise they can go in a fast sequence. Use a mirror.

STEP 3   ■ *Breathe in cool air on a whispered "kaa" with a full yawn-stretch. Picture the air going down to the breathing center.*

Release warm vibrations from the center on "hi" (as in "high" not "hit") letting them travel up and over the stretched soft palate, the roof of the mouth, the top teeth and out into the air.

Move the back of the tongue up and down underneath the soft palate, the resultant sound being "hi-yi-yi-yi." Keep the tip of the tongue touching the bottom teeth.

In this exercise you are allowing the sound the experience of escaping through a much larger channel than usual. The larger channel should stimulate a larger release from the source giving the opportunity for tasting a larger sense of freedom than before. At the same time you are incorporating a version of the tongue-loosening device so that you do not start to push in a habitual response to larger impulses.

  ■ *Practice Step 3 using a mirror to check that the soft palate remains up and stretched throughout the whole "sentence" of the exercise.*

Then practice it on ascending pitches, breathing in on "kaa" each time and sighing out the vibrations very freely.

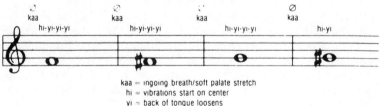

kaa = ingoing breath/soft palate stretch
hi = vibrations start on center
yi = back of tongue loosens

STEP 4   ■ *Let everything relax.*

Imagine there is someone you know outside the window, across a street, or a field, or a river, and call to him or her on "HI-I-I-I." Let the impulse to call come from your breathing/feeling center and let your throat/soft palate open to allow the call free passage.

STEP 5 ■ Let everything relax.

Without trying to lift the soft palate or attempting to apply anything of the previous four steps, return to the tongue exercise, Step 4.

Observe whether you feel any new vibrations or different spaces. As you go higher see whether (without consciously lifting it) the soft palate responds, providing new paths for the higher pitches. Is it easier to go higher?

STEP 6 ■ Roll your head on a hum and be aware of the soft palate and the back of the tongue. The space between them should be constantly changing as you roll. When your head is dropped back there is more space, when your head is forward there is less space, but the soft palate and the back of the tongue should never touch each other as you hum.

■ Drop down your spine on a hum looking for any differences there may be in the quality or disposition of the vibrations. Build up your spine, humming, and release the sound at the top.

■ Speak "huh-hummmmmmuh."

■ You should sense more natural space in your mouth/throat cavity than before. You may feel vibrations coming from that cavity. You should feel in general that there are more vibrations as a result of the greater space. Take advantage of whatever greater sense of freedom this gives.

■ When you come back to the tongue and humming exercises, allow the soft palate to adjust automatically as it chooses. Do not attempt to keep it lifted or you will end up sounding false, plum-voiced and pompous.

The throat

In dealing with the soft palate, you have also been dealing with the throat. When you yawn the stretch is not restricted to the soft palate but affects a mass of pharyngeal muscle as well. Properly speaking, I should refer to the *pharynx* from now on, but since it is not a word in common usage I shall use *throat* most of the time, meaning the part of the channel that runs behind the soft palate from the height of the nose down to the collar bone. The throat contains the larynx and provides the primary resonating cavities in the space between it and the back of the neck. The back wall of the throat is lined with muscle tissue which reacts to changing pitch with a toning response that tunes the pharyngeal cavity to give resonating feedback appropriate to that pitch. The resonating aspect of the throat will be explored more fully in the next chapter. Here, the interest is in the throat as part of a free channel for sound.

The main working point here is the sharp angle where the throat passage turns into the mouth passage. If the soft palate is lazy and the tongue tense, this quickly becomes a traffic jam corner. (See A.) Behind and below this corner the throat should be pictured, for working purposes, as a wide, unblocked passageway all the way down to the diaphragm. The less interest taken in the larynx the better.

The only work to be done with the throat at this point is to clear the traffic jam, stimulate the sensation of spaciousness, and explore the experience of a more direct and untrammeled connection with the breathing center as the channel frees.

A

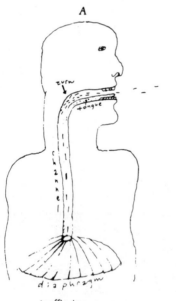

. . . *traffic jam corner*

B

. . . *no traffic jam*

STEP 1 ■ *Drop your head as far back as it will go easily without involving your shoulders, and see how the picture of the channel changes in this position. (See B.)*

There is now a straight column through which breath or sound can flow unimpeded from the diaphragm to the sky. No corners to turn; no traffic jam.

■ *In this position sigh out a whispered "haaaa."*
Using the back of the neck, bring the head up on top of the spine. Visualize the shape of the column now that the head is up, and sigh from center a whispered "hu-u-u-uh."

When the head is dropped back it is almost impossible to use the throat to support the sound, the breath must take over. You can, in this position, have a very distinct impression of the connection with the breathing center. When the head comes up again maintain that impression so that the connection is graphically clear as you release breath into the whispered "huh" and realize that, despite the angle the breath must now turn, there still need be no interference in the throat.

STEP 2 ■ *Drop the head back as before. Think of the tongue and jaw as belonging to the front of your body, and the soft palate and skull to the back of your body. Picture a wide chasm between your front and your back. At the very bottom of the chasm is a warm pool of vibrations.*
Release vibrations from the pool up through the chasm like a geyser: "haaaaaaaaa."

The throat remains totally uninvolved. The impulse for sound should be felt springing powerfully from a center of energy down below.

■ *Bring the head up on the back of the neck. The chasm changes its shape but it does not close.*
Release vibrations from the unchanged warm pool of vibrations below: "hu-uh-uh-uh."

As you continue to relax the throat and remove its ability to support sound, you should find your connection with the center of your breathing becoming clearer. Think of this center as the center of your energy.

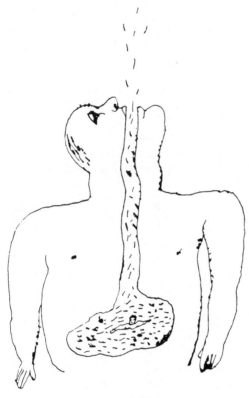

. . . a pool of vibrations

■ Repeating the first part of this step, this time focus your attention both on the starting point of sound in your center and on a spot on the ceiling (or in the sky) to which you want the vibrations to travel. Release "haaaaaaa" from the central pool of energy/vibrations and picture an unbroken stream of sound flowing all the way up through your body, through the air to the chosen arrival point.

■ Bring the head up — don't let the channel close — pick a spot straight ahead of you (a person if possible) and release vibrations from the warm central store to that arrival point.

■ Drop your head back. Imagine the pool of vibrations has a color. If one does not immediately occur to you, try blue. Release a long blue stream "haaaaaaaa" of blue vibrations to paint the ceiling blue, or to join the sky.

■ Bring the head up. Release your vibrations of color (perhaps in this position they change color) to paint the wall or the person opposite you "hu-uh-uh-uh."

■ Repeat any or all of the tongue, soft palate, humming exercises in conjunction with (1) your increased connection with the breathing/energy center, (2) your awareness of a relaxed throat, and (3) colors in the vibrations of sound (if they stimulate you).

The use of colors helps initially to bring some life into the sound. The mind and the imagination are more actively involved and the sounds begin to have some content, are not empty vibrations for their own sake. If you begin to use your imagination in this way you may find that different colors evoke different feelings in you. Experiment with them to find how to use them best; which are more peaceful, which more stimulating. But make sure you visualize them centrally, connecting with your feeling in the solar plexus or lower. You can get lost in inventive doodling if the colors emanate from the head level.

Part two:
The developing process:
the resonating ladder

You have now, in theory at least, freed the breathing process and therewith the source of sound, and you have also liberated the channel for sound through the relaxation of tensions in the jaw, the tongue and the throat. In practice you may have only become dimly aware of some of the components of your vocal apparatus, making occasional, haphazard contact with them. In theory, you cannot go on to develop your voice safely until you have freed it, but in practice you cannot wait for such a perfect process, so you will now proceed with the development and you will find that you further the liberation at the same time.

The development will be in two main areas: range and power. We will be starting with range because that increases the power as a by-product.

All the work will be based on the assumption that you can isolate resonating cavities throughout the body and increase the vibrations in those cavities. In physical fact, the exercises are perhaps diversionary, and employ the mind in such a way that the muscles governing the vocal folds are strengthened and the folds themselves function more and more efficiently. As the mind becomes conscious of the three to four octaves of range available in the speaking voice and of the endless variety of resonating quality within that range, the breath and vocal folds become more refined and strengthened in their response.

Since the physiological facts are difficult to work on directly, in the next body of exercises you will be asked to work to develop the voice through the actual resonators, which are a series of cavities differing widely in shape. Inside them exist vibrations appropriate to the amplification of different parts of the vocal range. I shall use as clear a set of working pictures as I can, and any devices possible — diagrams, imagination, emotion, analogy, absurdity or fact — to simplify and make tangible a complex coordination of the involuntary nervous system with a highly sophisticated acoustical mechanism.

Having forestalled any over-scientific criticism at the risk of arousing some misgivings, here is the description of the resonating ladder. Each note in the voice has its own resonating rung on the ladder, and the ladder is the body from the chest to the top of the skull. It is convenient to measure the voice in terms of the Western scale, giving it an average 3 octaves (though a more Eastern musical system would be truer because it is more subtle).

In the following exercises you will be directing your voice to move up and down the resonating ladder until every part of it is available, familiar and safe. Weak rungs can be strengthened, and gaps in the ladder can be filled in in ways that are physically palpable. The experience of your vocal range should be as physically concrete as possible. There need be no mysteries.

8: The channel resonators

We will begin with two large resonating cavities, the chest and the mouth, but before working with sound it is necessary to do some purely physical preparation exercises.

STEP 1   ■ *Drop your head back as in the throat-freeing exercise and picture the resulting wide passage down into the chest. This time imagine it spreading out into the rib cage as though into a great, hollow cave.*

■ *Focus clearly on the back of the neck, and being sure you are not using any jaw muscle strength and that your stomach muscles do not tighten at all, stretch up through the top seven vertebrae that comprise your neck until your head floats on top of the topmost vertebra. Notice that the passage has changed its shape but has not closed.*

■ *Drop your head forward without letting your mouth close. Notice that the passage has again changed its shape but that it need not close although the opening in this position is very narrow.*

■ *Bring the top seven vertebrae of the neck up into alignment with the rest of the spine, the head floating on top. Leave the jaw muscles loose enough for the jaw to drop slightly as the head comes up. The space between the teeth is a little wider than it was when the head was forward.*

■ *Drop the neck back, leaving the bottom jaw behind so that the wide passage from the throat down into the chest appears again.*

The primary action here is to shift all the responsibility for moving the head into the top seven vertebrae of the spine (the back of the neck). The by-product of this action as the neck moves from front to back is that the shape of the channel automatically changes as the relationship between the skull and jaw changes. This spontaneous response depends on complete freedom in the jaw hinges and as it is possible that there is still some tension there you may, for the time being, have to drop the jaw consciously when you bring the neck up from the forward position and over to the back.

■ *Practice Step 1 until you feel you have made strong contact with the back of the neck and that you can move it through the three positions without any tightening in the stomach muscles. Put your hand on your stomach and insist that your breathing continues in a natural easy rhythm as your head drops back and forward.*

STEP 2 ■ *Drop your neck back and, as in Step 2 of the throat exercises, find a pool of vibrations deep inside and sigh out on "haaaaaaaa." Let it be a low, very relaxed, warm, easy sound. Make sure it is all vibration, not breathy at all.*
Put your hand on your chest and register the vibrations of that sound throughout the chest.
Repeat the sounds:

> *haaaa haaaa haaaa ∅*
> *haaaa haaaa haaaa haaaa haaaa ∅*
> *haa haa haa haa haa ∅*

■ *Bring the back of the neck up, head floating on top: Know that the shape of the channel has changed but not closed, and allow the sound to flow into the mouth cavity on "hu-uh-uh."*
Let the pitch rise a little and you will find the sound that awakens a definite sensation of vibrations all through the roof of the mouth and the teeth. Repeat the sounds until you find resonating feedback from the bony mouth cavity:

> *hu-u-uh hu-u-uh hu-u-uh ∅*
> *huh-huh-huh-huh-huh ∅*
> *huh-huh-huh ∅*

■ *Drop the neck back again, this time as though you are removing the mouthbox resonator from the picture, leaving yourself only with the lower throat and chest resonators.*
Find a low sound on "haaaaaa" that rumbles round the chest cavities. Indulge and wallow in the sound. Go as deep as you can without pushing down in the throat in any way.

Beat your chest with your fists to shake up and awaken more vibrations.

- Bring the neck up again, picturing the mouthbox resonator restored as the head floats up.

Find a sound and a pitch that will awaken the optimum resonating feedback from the bony walls of the mouthbox.

- Go from mouth resonator (neck straight) to chest resonator (neck back) and back again several times:

  huh-huh-huh-huh-huh   ∅
  drop neck back
  haa-haa-haa-haa-haa   ∅
  neck up
  huh-huh-huh-huh-huh   ∅
  neck back
  haa-haa-haa-haa-haa   ∅

Observe the change of pitch and the completely different quality of resonance in each cavity.

- Go from chest resonator to mouth resonator, and then drop the neck forward.

The channel is now very narrow and sound falling forward through it will arrive, shaped by the channel into "heeeeee," on the front teeth.

Feel the vibrations on the front teeth and find the pitch (slightly higher than the mouth pitch) that awakens the clearest resonating feedback from the front teeth.

- Now travel the head from the front, to the top, to the back, using only the back of the neck to move it. Allow the shape of the resonating channel to change as spontaneously as possible in response to the changing relationship of the skull and jaw and release a flow of vibrations from center that focuses on the front teeth, the mouth and the chest according to the altering shape of the channel:

  hee-hee-hee   (front teeth vibrations: neck forward)
  huh-huh-huh   (mouth vibrations: neck straight)
  haa-haa-haa   (chest vibrations: neck back)
  haa-haa-haa   (low pitch: chest resonance)
  huh-huh-huh   (middle pitch: mouth resonance)
  hee-hee-hee   (slightly higher: front teeth resonance)

There is a fine distinction in this exercise between placing the sound in the different resonators and letting it happen there as a result of other, causal conditions. To begin with, you will certainly have to think "haa" "huh" "hee" and think about changing the pitch from lower to higher. Try, however, to think of this exercise in terms of the "let it happen" concept, that may not yet hold true, due to residual tensions but should be continually borne in mind.

The first observation to make is that when your head is back and your throat wide open, the only sound that can happen without you changing the shape and without moving an extra muscle, is "haa," so the shape dictates the vowel and the vowel is the by-product of the shape. When your neck straightens, the head comes up and the jaws swing into their median position; if the tongue is completely relaxed, the only sound that can happen without changing the shape of the channel and without moving an extra muscle, is "huh." (This can be difficult to experience because of lurking tensions in the back of the tongue which secretly distort the shape.) When you drop your head forward and the channel narrows, if the tongue is relaxed so that it falls forward but does not block the opening, the only sound that can happen without changing the shape or moving a muscle is "hee."

■ *With a heightened awareness of the condition of the channel in the three positions, go through them once more with one long sigh of breath only (no sound) from center. You may hear the whispered "haa, huh, hee" as the breath is automatically molded on its way out through the changing channel.*

Do not linger over this point if you do not get a completely satisfactory result. What I have described depends on totally free breathing and a totally free jaw, tongue and throat.

The second observation of the *"let it happen"* concept is that pitch, within the exercise, will also change spontaneously as the structure changes its shape. Larger spaces create a lower frequency of vibrations than smaller ones. Eventually all you need do is provide a steady supply of vibrations from center, and as the head and neck move through the three main positions, those vibrations will automatically rise from lower to higher because the cavity gets smaller.

This concept, however, is a refinement, and for the time being it is enough to awaken the voice to three major resonating areas using whatever is necessary to experience some of the different qualities of vibration resounding from different surfaces.

STEP 3   In order to provide a stimulus for the breathing center, which may be suffering from neglect as the attention moves elsewhere, try the whole sequence again with a new image behind it.

■ *Drop the head back, throat wide.*
This time imagine the throat widening down into the chest as an old-fashioned chimney widening down to a fireplace. In the big, old-fashioned fireplace there is a large fire warming you in your

middle. Picture yourself sitting in a comfortable armchair beside the fire, feeling relaxed and warm. Let the warmth of the fire and your feeling of contentment release on a deep, warm "haaaa" all the way up and out of the chimney.

■ Keep in touch with your fire. Bring the head and neck up. The chimney changes its shape but does not close. Let the warmth of the fire release to warm the roof of the mouth on "hu-u-uh."

■ Drop your head and neck forward. Keep in touch with the fire feeling. Let the warmth and vibration stream on to your front teeth "heee." (The "heat" is more focused and sharper in this position.)

■ Head up, "huh-huh-huh," (a warm spot focused on the roof of the mouth).

■ Head back; relax back down by the fire; let the warmth spread all through the torso "haaaa haaaa."

STEP 4 ■ Repeat the exercise with a different image. This time imagine you have a store of paint in your breathing area. Perhaps spray cans of paint with buttons in the diaphragm.

Head back / chest resonance / paint a great swatch of purple on the ceiling "haaaaaa."

Head up / mouth resonance / paint a large blob of royal blue on the opposite wall "huh," / then three blobs "huh-huh-huh."

Head forward / teeth resonance / paint a thin line of bright green on the floor from your middle "heeeee."

Reverse the process going from green to blue to purple.

■ Keep the paint coming from your middle. See the colors arrive where you aim them. Notice the resonators as a by-product of your game.

It is worth spending a great deal of time with these basic channel resonance exercises. First get familiar with the concept and the general picture, then develop variations of your own within the concept. You may experience different energy content in each area, particularly when you are playing with colors, and there are intrinsically different energies with changes of pitch. It is a sign of increased organic awareness when you begin to apprehend the connection between energy and resonating response, and you may want to experiment with mood or feeling content within the given framework.

STEP 5 When you have become thoroughly familiar with the resonating jumps from chest to mouth to teeth you can begin to fill in the rungs of pitch.

■ Introduce the picture of the resonating ladder and think of walking up through the chest and throat, rung by rung, over the soft palate, into the roof of the mouth, over the upper gum ridge and onto the front teeth. Let the voice travel upward in pitch in even intervals, each interval finding its appropriate resonating rung. This should be explored in speaking inflections, not sung.

■ Find out how much variety there is within each general resonating area by setting up imaginary conversations: Within the chest resonating area entirely on "haa"'s (a scene based on relaxed, contented circumstances would provide the most appropriate energy); within the mouth resonating area entirely on "huh"'s (a scene containing more urgency and life); within the resonating area of the front teeth on "hee"'s (here let increasing interest engender an excitement of energy to fill the sounds that spring from center to teeth).

This isolation of resonating cavities is practiced in order to develop parts of the vocal range that might otherwise lie dormant. In natural speaking such isolated response is rare and will occur only in the case of a locked emotional state or extreme tension. In normal use there is a blend of vibrations from several resonating areas and a constantly changing proportion of higher and lower overtones according to the changing intensity of the thought/feeling content.

STEP 6   Here the aim is to free yourself through your voice on a call. Do not try consciously to incorporate the work you have just done on the resonators, but be aware as you call of the blend of vibration from chest, mouth and front teeth.

■ Let the impulse to call originate in the breathing center.
Let the objective be to free yourself.
The sound is a long, easy, unforced "hey."

■ Let the jaw, the tongue, the throat, be completely relaxed and let the call spring from the energy center of the solar plexus/diaphragm as you free yourself on a long
    he-e-e-e-ey
that gathers vibrations from all available resonating surfaces in the chest, throat, soft palate, roof of mouth, teeth, on its way out of your body to the far distance.

9: Releasing the voice from the body

Most of the emphasis in the preceding exercises has been on a physical awareness that can permit specific routing of impulses from the mind to stimulate new areas of physical response and de-activate old habitual responses. In working with such consciousness it is not easy to feel free, at the same time, yet that is the overall aim of this work: *To liberate the natural voice and yourself with it.* This chapter offers some very easy general ways of releasing the voice from the body with more emphasis on *what* you are releasing than *how*. The only image to retain is that of sound emanating from the *center* of the body. By now the concept of a center for the voice should be familiar as the physical source of sound in the center of the diaphragm, and the impulse center in the solar plexus region. This should not deny any sensations you may have of the voice and/or the energy originating deeper down in the torso.

STEP 1 ■ *Set up a simple scenario in your mind's eye. For example: You are standing on the sidewalk of a busy street and you see someone you know on the other side whose attention you wish to catch. Or: You look out through a window and across a garden. You see someone you know and are surprised to see there.*

■ *In response to either scene you call out on "hey" or "hi" to your friend.*

■ *Think through the scene in clearly defined steps. For example:*

You look out of the window to see what the weather is like.
You see your friend. (A specific person and one you like.)
What you see fills you with the need to call to him or her.
You release the call.
You relax, breathe, and wait for the reaction.

Throughout the scene your body is acted on: first by the outside stimulus, then by the desire to communicate. There should therefore be no need to push or strain in order to call.

Practice feeding the desire to call down into the center and releasing that desire through a free channel.

STEP 2   ■ *Remove the image of calling to someone and easily sigh a long "he-e-e-ey" out from the center.*

■ *As you free your voice on "he-e-ey" gently bounce your shoulders up and down shaking the sound as it flows out.*

■ *Then bounce your whole body loose on "he-e-e-ey." Let the knees bend loosely and straighten in an easy, bouncy movement, let the arms be loose, shoulders loose, stomach muscles loose, head loose, jaw loose as you bounce a loose, long sound out of your body.*

■ *Imagine that there are springs under the soles of your feet and that the rest of your body is like a loose-jointed marionette. Start the "he-e-e-ey" in the center and bounce on the springs all over the room, your body flapping everywhere and the sound flying out of you quite uncontrolled. Don't preserve the sound at all, let it be utterly influenced by the shaking out of your body.*

■ *Stand still. Start "hey"'s in the center and slowly drop down through your spine until you are hanging head downward with the "hey"'s dropping out through the top of your loosely hanging head in response to gravity. Let the Breath replace easily, and then slowly come up the spine calling "hey"'s. Let there be a new breath whenever you need it. When you reach the top, decide to abandon yourself in a long, releasing, pleasurable "he-e-e-ey."*

■ *Lie on your back on the floor. Go through your body to relax all tensions and then call "he-e-ey" freely from center to the ceiling.*

■ *Roll over on your stomach. Put your forehead on your hands so that your face is toward the floor. Sigh with relief several times deep into your body. Notice that in this position the spine lengthens down toward the feet as you breathe in deeply, and shortens as you breathe out. The small of the back lifts on an incoming breath and drops on* an outgoing breath. With this awareness, call "he-e-eey" from the prone position.

You can try many of the preceding exercises lying face down on the floor. It is a position that immediately reveals any unnecessary head movements implying tension in the back of the neck or jaw. The sounds can be pictured more graphically as *falling* forward and out of the mouth in response to gravity. (And once you get the feeling of breath affecting the lower spine you are less likely to slip back into shallow breathing without noticing.)

■ *Roll loosely from lying on your stomach to lying on your back; to your stomach, to your back, while letting loose, easy sounds be released from your body. Let your whole body be sloppy. Be sure there is no holding in the jaw, neck or throat. Don't protect or preserve the sound in any way. Each time the body falls heavily onto the stomach or heavily onto the back, the sound should be bumped out by the impact. Try to do this out of doors, rolling down a grassy hill.*

You can use any or all of these physical loosenings to advantage while doing a speech or a poem. Choose something you know well and whose content you can stay with. Let your attention focus 100% on the thoughts and feelings of what you are saying but get rid of any possible physical tension that may accompany the performance by shaking out your body, in one of the seven ways suggested, while you speak. You will have to sacrifice many of the external results you might have established hitherto for a particular piece. All your inflections will be shaken out, all your external controls removed. Take advantage of this. Be concerned only with the inner content and let that come from you in new ways that you had not planned at all. You may be surprised to find meanings and feelings which come to you out of the blue as your body frees you from habitual thought patterns and emotional ruts.

Intermission: Working plan for material in chapters 3 through 9

At this stage of working on yourself through work on your voice, you should be able to plan a twenty to thirty minute run-through of exercises to be done regularly before learning new ones, before any rehearsal of a play or a scene, before an acting class or before an actual performance. You have accumulated the contents of a vocal warm-up; Partial as yet, but effective.

I would remind you that these movements and sounds are designed to help recondition your whole way of communicating and that such reconditioning takes time and constant reprogramming before it sticks and the communicating process forms reliable new habits. Old habits and daily tension fight hard to be retained and these exercises are for daily use until the actor retires or decides to open a candy store or raise hogs instead of struggling with theatre.

Here is the outline of a suggested warm-up; all the exercises have been described in detail in the previous chapters.

Warm-up (30 minutes)

Physical awareness (no sound)

- *Stretch and drop down the spine.*
Build up.
Roll the head and neck.

With your hands loosen your jaw.
Stretch and relax the tongue.

Limber the soft palate.
Yawn and stretch all over.
Roll the head.
Drop down the spine again — build up.

(approximately 5 minutes)

Breathing ■ *Stand with awareness of alignment and balance*
Close your eyes and be aware of the skeleton.
*Turn your attention inward and be aware of your everyday rhythm
of breathing.*
Allow the breath to release on small "fff"'s.
Repeat several times until involuntary rhythm takes over.

(approximately 2 minutes)

Touch of sound ■ *Central awareness of vibrations on*
huh-huh

(approximately 1 minute)

Vibrations ■ *Lip vibrations*
huh-hummmmmmmuh
Move lips around on vibrations.
Blow out through lips.
Move top lip up and down (sneer).
Move bottom lip up and down.
Stretch them sideways with your fingers in the corners. Let them go.
Blow out through your lips on sound βμμμμ
Repeat several times going down one tone at a time on pitch.
Repeat
huh-hummmmmmuh
on descending pitches

(approximately 4 minutes)

Roll your head on a hum.
Alternate directions, changing pitches, 6 or 7 times.
Drop down your spine on a hum.
Come up and release sound at the top.
Repeat several times on descending and ascending pitches
huh-hummmmmmh (speak it).

(approximately 4 or 5 minutes)

Tongue ■ *Sigh out from center and loosen tongue*
hee-yuh-yuh-yuh-yuh-yuh

Repeat on ascending and descending pitches
    hee-yuh-yuh-yuh
    hee-yuh-yuh-yuh
Repeat it hanging head down and building up the spine (to relax the breathing muscles).

(approximately 1½ minutes)

Soft palate   ■ *Breathe in and out on whispered "kaa," stretching soft palate into yawn-stretch.*
Sigh out from center over stretched soft palate on ascending and descending pitches
    hi-yi-yi-yi
moving the back of the tongue up and down to relax it.
Call on "hi."

(approximately 1½ minutes)

Throat   ■ *Drop head back to free throat and find connection with center*
    haaaa

(approximately ½ minute)

Resonators   ■ *Experience chest, mouth, front teeth vibrations with, respectively, head dropped back*
    haaaa haaa haaa
neck straight, head up
    huh huh huh
head forward
    heee heee heee
Reverse the process, then alternate it, from front to back and vice-versa.
Repeat with colors and/or imagined scenes.

(approximately 3 minutes)

Freeing   ■ *Call to free yourself*
    he-e-e-e-ey
Shake the "hey" out, bouncing the shoulders, the knees, the whole body. Jumping.
Roll your head around calling
Drop down your spine calling

(approximately 2 minutes)

Floor work   ■ *Lie on your back, on your stomach.*
Repeat any of the exercises for greater relaxation.

10: The middle of the voice

We are now moving into the most subtle, complex, and interesting part of the voice. It is halfway up the resonating ladder, and in the middle register. This can be the most revealing area of a voice, and perhaps for that reason it becomes the least freely used. The resonating corridors here are labyrinthine compared with the simple chest, pharynx and mouth chambers. You have to examine an actual skull to appreciate how many and how varied in shape are the passages and chambers within the mask of the face. Some are scooped out of solid bone, some are a millimeter wide and have walls of transparent cartilage. With such multiplicity of shape and texture there is endless potential variety in resonating quality. And yet when most people use their middle register, they employ one or two notes, sometimes strident, sometimes nasal, sometimes breathy, sometimes sing-y, but seldom with more than one over-riding quality. Even when the sound is very pleasant to listen to because it is "well-placed" and "well-modulated," it will not express more than just that: a well-trained voice. I find a well-trained voice hard to trust for it implies a well-trained person who knows how he or she wants to be perceived and can achieve what is desired. A person who has enough control to present a consistently "pleasant" tone of voice is hiding many things.

With the variety of resonating qualities available it is possible for the most subtle nuances of thought to be revealed accurately. How dangerous that can be in daily human commerce is evidenced by how rarely they are heard. Easily triggered defense mechanisms develop early in life to make the most revealing part of the voice the best guarded. The vocal defense network is set up through mental cross-currents which create harmonics of pitch and resonance and concomitant tensions in the face muscles. Some of the defensive reactions are instinctual and spontaneous, some instinctual hardening to habitual; some are semiconscious character choices, some imitative. All result in muscle responses that block access to certain resonating chambers and divert vibrations into others. The primary resonating response is checked and secondary ones convey a veiled message.

I'll give an example of this: In a comment such as "Darling, I think you're driving too fast" there might be a primary feeling impulse of fear, modified by a characteristic of staying calm in a crisis. The energy stimulated by fear would, if expressed directly, activate the breath and the vocal folds to produce a relatively high frequency of vibration which in turn would find amplification in resonators in the middle to upper part of the face. Myriads of tiny muscles in the tissue lining the upper pharynx, the soft palate and the upper sinuses would pick up the energy of the initial impulse, creating muscle tone capable of feeding back more vibrations of the same frequency, thereby relaying accurately the primary fear stimulus.

Tuned-up emotional vibrations generate tuned-up sound vibrations, unless countermanded by a stream of secondary messages from character elements or external influences. In the case of the dangerous driver, the actual sequence of psycho-physical reactions in the passenger might be:

1. Stab of panic in the solar plexus stimulating a swift intake of breath, and a simultaneous, almost imperceptible tightening in the temples, eyeballs, scalp muscles, upper pharynx.

2. Conditioned, therefore speedy, decision not to express the panic. Habitual depression of the back of the tongue and larynx in order to create a passageway down into the deep, calm resonating area of the chest.

3. Manipulation of the laryngeal musculature and lower register to convey in a warm, deep tone the gentle suggestion that it is better to be safe than sorry, to be late than dead — anything that might help reduce the speed.

Another kind of character-conditioning might just as easily take the fear impulse and turn it into laughter; possibly a rather high giggly laughter as those particular character influences add impulses that increase the tension of the muscle response and spiral everything, including the sound, higher.

Innumerable variations can be played on this one simple example by adding different ingredients. The driver's state of mind; the relationship between the two; the frequency of the incident; the reality of the danger, and so on. They are all more commonly expressed than the basic, simple (as opposed to complex) fear impulse. Until the actor's voice can express pure unadulterated feelings it cannot be relied on to express complexities with any accuracy. The complexities the actor chooses, or the role demands, will be filtered through unchosen admixtures of habitual defenses and individual characteristics, and will emerge sounding quite different from what the mind had conceived.

In summary, a concept of pure connection of thought and feeling energy with breath, vibration and resonating response underlies this exploration of range. You can do it by treating the voice as a musical instrument, sound only, divorced from feeling, but you can also open your mind to the wedding of feeling with sound, and allow them to be mutually stimulating.

The following exercises will provide some clues as to how to make all the mask resonators available. Do not think of the mask in terms of a Halloween mask or Commedia mask, with just the dimensions you can see when you look in a mirror. Meditate a little on its inner dimensions, its depth behind the nose, and the bony catacombs hidden by the skin.

First you must activate and limber up all the muscles of the face which run vertically, horizontally and diagonally. These can either mobilize to aid communication or immobilize to block it.

Physical preparation for work on the middle of the voice

Face Isolations

■ *Lift and lower the right eyebrow several times.*

Lift and lower the left eyebrow several times.

Lift and lower the right cheek several times.

Lift and lower the left cheek several times.

Lift and lower the upper lip several times.

Lift and lower the lower lip several times.

Stretch the right corner of the mouth sideways and release it.

Stretch the left corner of the mouth sideways and release it.

Alternate stretching the right and left corners of the mouth.

Wrinkle the bridge of the nose up and release it.

Move the bridge of the nose up and down.

Squeeze the right eye shut.

Stretch the right eye open.

Squeeze the left eye shut.

Stretch the left eye open.

Alternate vigorously opening and shutting the right & left eye.

■ *Lift the left eyebrow up stretch the right corner of the mouth sideways simultaneously.*

Release.

Lift the right eyebrow up stretch the left corner of the mouth sideways simultaneously.

Release.

■ *Devise any combination of movements to stretch the face vertically, horizontally and diagonally. Make intentional movements and check them in a mirror to see whether you are connecting as you think you are.*

■ *Finally: squeeze the whole face into a tight ball.*

Stretch the whole face as wide as it can go (eyes and mouth wide).

Shake the skin of the face off the bones.

Massage your face with your hands.

The middle sinus resonators

Sinus means a recess, cavity or hollow space. A hollow space scooped out of bone makes a perfect resonating cavity and the following work will focus on the two most familiar pairs of sinus cavities, those on either side of the nose which I shall call the middle sinuses, and those above the nose and eyebrows, the upper sinuses.

STEP 1 ■ *With your fingers feel the shape of your face from the nose out to the cheekbones. You will find a slight hollow between the two bony hills of nose and cheeks which is soft and spongy, sometimes sensitive. Gently massage this area with your fingertips, in small circles moving up and outward from the nostrils.*

■ *Now move the middle sinus area up and down with its own muscles. This is the movement you might use to push a slipping pair of eyeglasses back up on the bridge of the nose.*

STEP 2 ■ *Let your mouth drop open just enough for a whispered "heeee" to be formed automatically when you release breath through the narrow space. The tongue must be loose and somewhat far forward in the mouth for this to happen spontaneously.*

■ Sigh a sustained "heeee" through your mouth on a mid-register pitch (approximately an F above middle C) and at the same time massage the middle sinuses with your fingertips.

Let the breath drop back into center and release another "heeee" one note higher. Massage the sinus area. Repeat for several ascending notes.

■ Sigh out another "heeee" (going higher until you feel you have to push, then coming back down again) and this time move the sinus skin up and down with its own muscles. (This is the eyeglass shifting movement, wrinkling the bridge of the nose similar to the nose-wrinkling reaction to a strange smell).

Wrinkle, relax; wrinkle, relax on a sustained "heeeee."

■ Alternate massaging the sinuses and exercising the sinus muscles with the wrinkling-releasing as you think the pitch higher each time, coming down when either the breathing gets difficult or the throat gets tight.

You must keep aiming the "heeee" very deliberately out through the mouth. Do not let the sound be placed in the sinuses, although you are awakening vibrations in that area. If you aim the sound there it will arrive in the nose which will do no harm but will deny the exploration of the many other qualities of vibration to be found surrounding the nose.

A vital point of awareness in this exercise is the tongue. The back of the tongue, as explained earlier, commonly starts to tense as the voice goes higher, substituting its muscular strength for the support of breath. As the sinus resonators open up they will begin to provide resonating strength for the voice which can thus start to transfer its dependence from the back of the tongue to its true strengths of breath and resonance. The more you relax the tongue the more the voice will demand support from the breath and find its true resonators. The corollary of this is that the more the voice finds its true resonating power, the more the tongue can relax.

■ To prove that you are not relying on the tongue to boost the voice up the register, do the exercise in Step 3 with the tip of the tongue lying loosely on the lower lip. Put your thumb into the soft underside of the jaw and make sure that there is no hardening at all in the bottom of the tongue as you go higher.

STEP 3 ■ Let the tongue slide, thick and relaxed, forward and out of the mouth. (If it is really relaxed it will be wide, touching the corners *of the mouth, thick and unmoving. If it tenses anywhere along its length it will try to pull back into the mouth again, become pointed or thin and flat.)*

■ *Sigh out the "heeee" through your mouth and over your tongue through what is now a very narrow space between the surface of the tongue and the top teeth.*

■ *Move the sinuses up and down on the ascending "heeee"'s checking that the tongue stays totally relaxed throughout. Relax for a new breath.*

■ *Use this series of ascending "heeee"'s to check out the interrelationship of tongue and breath. If the tongue goes hard on the underside of the jaw area, massage it loose again with your fingers while continuing the sound. You can push upward into this area quite vigorously as it is insensitive. There should be the same soft condition as when you are silent, whatever the pitch. Whenever the tongue tightens, become aware of your breathing and sigh out with more release, more freedom, from deeper inside.*

For the basic freeing of the voice make a general rule: As you go higher, sigh deeper.

■ *Forgetting the specific focus of the preceding work, call freely on a long easy "he-e-e-ey." Shake the sound out — loosen through your whole body on sound.*

The reason for sighing more as you go higher is to break a common conditioned reflex of pushing for the high notes. Reaching, bracing, working harder or simply refusing are all common psycho-physical reactions to going up in pitch. If you consciously decide to sigh with more and more relief as you go higher you do three things: (a) you undo tensions that automatically assault the breathing muscles in preparation for the hard work ahead, because you cannot sigh tensely; (b) you deliver a greatly increased gust of breath to help impel and support the pitch; (c) you undermine the pushing, working, suffering and/or "I can't" syndrome by substituting a palpable sensation of relief which has to be allied with pleasure. If you can decide that it is a *sigh of pleasurable relief* and that each ascending pitch can connect with more and deeper pleasurable relief, then you will generate enormous energy, enormous quantities of breath, and a new attitude to high notes which will make them a great deal easier to produce.

Do not be anxious if the quality of the sound is not aesthetically satisfying at this stage. Be content to focus solely on causal things: The freedom of the breath in response to the thought of higher pitch, the loosening of the face muscles, the continued freedom in the throat, tongue and jaw. The results may be very strange initially, and it is sometimes better that they are, because your old aesthetic standards may have to give place to new. In the freeing stage of training, aesthetic judgment is usually an inhibiting factor and should be postponed to a much later, refining phase. As long as you are clinging to an aural criterion and inwardly commenting "that's a hideous sound," "I sound much better when I'm singing" or "that's not my voice," you may be sure you are not directing all your attention to the physical and sensory aspects of the work, and the results will never be satisfactory.

The reconditioning involved in meeting the demand of a higher and higher pitch is designed not only to help open up your range, or to develop your singing voice, though it will do both. It is also a basic reprogramming designed to change the response to all large demands on the voice from greater effort to greater release: The demand of a powerful character you must embody, the demand of a huge theatre you must be heard in, the demand of a powerful emotion that has to be communicated. Such powerful communication should be the by-product of abundant inner energies of the appropriate nature; open, free communicative channels of voice and body; a strong, generous desire to communicate and promise of the great pleasure inherent in such communication.

11: The nasal resonator

A clear distinction must be made between the terms nasal resonance and nasality. Nasality is the quality heard when, finding the opening into the mouth obscured, the voice escapes through the nose instead. The physical causes for nasality are a lazy soft palate which may sit flaccidly on the back of the tongue, and the tongue itself which can bunch up at the back, driving the sound sharply into the nose. Nasality inevitably implies torpid breathing. Nasality can be heard in deep voices, high voices or middle-register voices and means that the pall of a single resonating quality hangs over all utterance. When a deep voice is nasal it tends to be richly adenoidal and monotonous; when a medium-pitched voice is nasal it tends to be aggressively strident and monotonous, and when a high-pitched voice is nasal it is piercingly monotonous.

Nasal resonance, on the other hand, is a vital part of the whole resonating system. It provides brilliance and carrying power for the voice and is a major component of mask resonance. Its power must be tempered by balance, since it can easily dominate and distort the whole. Many actors have found that if they place their voices up in the nose/cheek-bone area they can be very easily heard in the back row of the balcony. So easily, in fact, that they need hardly exert themselves in any other respect. Being heard is only perhaps a third of the battle, and clear, empty voices often sail up to ears that hear the words and wonder what it's all about. Those whose aim is to share what they feel with an audience, will allow emotional energy to activate the breath and generate vibrations. These vibrations, reinforced by all possible resonating feedback, will flow out through the body, gathering a mix of mask and nasal vibrations as they travel through the face which create sound waves with a carrying power appropriate to the initial aim. Communication is a by-product of intention and freedom.

As with the other resonators, the nasal cavity should be discovered, isolated, developed and then left to react automatically in the general interplay of speech.

Be aware first of the shape of the nose bone and realize that vibrations arriving in that sharply concave structure will resound with great intensity. (If, for instance, you stand close to the corner of a room and make sounds into the angle, you get a much stronger resonating feedback than if you speak on to a flat wall.)

STEP 1 ■ *With your finger, press the right side of your nose to close off the right nostril. Breathe in through the other nostril in short, sharp, quick sniffs. Five or six sniffs should fill you up; then breathe out through your mouth on "ffff."*

Close off the left nostril with your finger and sniff sharply up the right nostril, five or six times, then let the breath out through the mouth.

■ *Repeat this several times for each nostril, registering the feeling of cold air in the nasal passages, and in the back of the throat behind the soft palate.*

STEP 2 ■ *Having sniffed up each nostril several times, rest, and be conscious of the cool places where the breath has rushed through. Then:*

Close off the right nostril and hum on a medium pitch, picturing the humming vibrations as flowing exclusively through the left nostril and warming the cool spots.

Close off the left nostril and hum, feeling the vibrations flowing through the right nostril.

Repeat several times on ascending notes.

■ *Do the same thing focusing the sound more into the bridge of the nose by wrinkling the nose up while humming.*

Wrinkle the bridge of the nose and while it is wrinkled breathe in and out through both nostrils.

Aim a hum where the wrinkle is and while humming, massage with your fingertips from the nostrils outward in small circles. Repeat on ascending pitches, a new breath between each, the hum becoming stronger and more focused into the nose as you massage.

■ Now, aiming the sound 100% into the nose, let the hum turn from a focused "mmmmmmmm" into a narrow "meeeee" with the "eeee" coming exclusively through the nose.

Repeat it—"mee-mee-mee"—aiming into the wrinkled bridge of the nose, aware that the sound is coming up into the nose from behind the soft palate, none of it releasing into the mouth.

Relax. Drop down the spine. Roll your head.

■ Repeat the "mee"'s into the nose on ascending pitches going at least from an A above middle C to the E above that.

Speak the "mee-mee-mee" into the nose on quite a high speaking pitch. Feel the vibrations ping into the nose.

■ Relax. Drop down the spine. Build up. Stretch and relax the tongue. Breathe in and out on a whispered "kaa" to release the soft palate. Then, forgetting the focus of the preceding exercises, call "he-e-ey," long and free from center. Shake out your body on sound.

Remembering that there is a correlation between increasing inner energy and ascending pitch, do not pull back from the strength of the intense, ringing vibrations the nose bone produces. To begin with you may feel you have to push slightly in your throat to get the sound focused sharply enough, but gradually you should find that you can transfer such effort from the body to the mind. The mental image of the path to the nasal cavity strengthens, the power of the thought of the sound increases, and the ability to bypass the throat completely develops.

I should like to comment here on an important point that I shall repeat later in other ways. The human voice is very resilient. If you treat it tentatively, always afraid of strain, you will never stretch it or tap its unknown potential, for you will always stay within what is safe and familiar. If you are tentative, you may think you are just being physically careful, but you will also be holding back on essential energies which are the very fuel the voice needs. Carefulness, thus, of the wrong sort, can create a vicious circle. By now it is worth taking the risk of occasionally scraping your throat or getting a little hoarse in order to find new possibilities. You now know enough to restore the voice to a good state if you happen to strain. If this should happen (and I must stress that it certainly need not ever happen), go through all the basic relaxation exercises with particular emphasis on the tongue and throat loosening. Then, gently humming, roll your head, drop down the spine, massage the face, and so on. Humming provides a natural massage for the vocal folds, and this treatment, administered as soon after the strain as possible, is much better for your voice than resting it by being silent. It is also healthier psychologically, removing the fear of "losing your voice," the very kind of energy-sapper that contributes most to the condition.

STEP 3 ■ *Wrinkle the bridge of the nose and again prepare the path by sniffing in and out.*
Send the "mee-mee-mee" pinging into the nose.

Put your fingertips on the bridge of the nose, and imagine that you can, with your fingers, draw the vibrations from the bridge of the nose across the cheekbones. Let the sound expand slightly from "mee-mee-mee" to a very narrow "mey-mey-mey." This sound must still come through the nose but is now influenced by an extended resonating surface. It fans out in opposite directions from a point on top of the bridge of the nose across the ridge of the upper cheekbones.

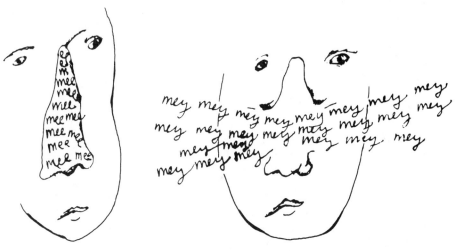

Relax your throat, soft palate and tongue and shake sound out generally from your whole body.

STEP 4 You are now going to redirect the vibrations from your nose into your mouth. The idea to work with is that having developed an intensely packed crowd of vibrations in your nose you are now going to free them out through the mouth. They will still be nasal vibrations, but will go through the mouth instead of the nose. In order for this to happen, the soft palate trap door, which has automatically closed in response to your direction that sound be diverted into the nose, must fly open at the appropriate moment, restoring the mouth channel.

■ *Send the "mee"'s into the bridge of the nose as before. Spread the vibrations across the cheekbones on the "mey"'s as before.*
Then, (and this is where the soft palate flies open) send the vibrations consciously out through the mouth on "mah-mah-mah."
Relax — breathe.

- Repeat the whole sequence on one breath on ascending pitches

  mee-mee-mee-mey-meY-mEY-MAH-MAH-MAAAAH

  (nose)   (cheekbones)   (mouth)

Find the pitch that evokes the strongest resonating feedback from each area — it will be quite high.

- Speak the whole sequence on a high speaking pitch which uses the same resonance as you found when singing. This may be a little higher when it is in the nose and a little lower when in the mouth but be sure to remain on a pitch that finds the optimum resonating feedback from the nose. Find the correlating pitch for that specific resonator and then free that pitch and that resonance through the mouth. It is easy to make the mistake of dropping into the pitch appropriate to the mouth resonance or lower.

Relax; breathe, shake out.

This is a difficult part of the voice to discover and, having made it available, to understand. It is on the way from the middle, much-used part of the register to the very high, excited part in the skull whose use can be easily understood in terms of expressing high energy states and obviously hysterical states. The rungs on the resonating ladder leading from the bridge of the nose to the forehead are often skipped completely in vocal development, and it is usually here that the famous "break" in the singing voice, that everyone asks about sooner or later, occurs.

In my observation it seems to be the most vulnerable part of the voice. I do not mean the weakest. It expresses the most ingenuous, open, vulnerable feelings and thoughts. It is there to respond to quivering, naked fears, to innocent surprise, to sudden, amazed joy, to naive, open questions that go up at the end. (It is surprising how few questions are asked with a simple, rising inflection. Start listening and you may hear how many have a preconceived answer implicit in them that turns the inflection away from vulnerability.) As is the case with vulnerable areas, this part of the vocal register has become guarded. High-octane impulses are rerouted away from it, and although such impulses may send the pitch into the upper register, the resonating response will be more safely found in the nose, or it will be reduced to half by an excessive rush of breath. When such energy-impulses end up in the nose they are extremely piercing and unendearing; the decoy of excess volume is an interesting defense against direct response. The opposite method is the breathy reaction where the words are heard through a misty filter suggesting the defense of appeasement: "Look how weak and unprotected I am — I dare not even commit my thoughts to a whole voice. In a way I hope you won't quite hear what I have to say in case I'm wrong."

To give some example of what I mean, here are three versions of the same scene:

Two people who were in love with each other ten years ago, and haven't met since, meet suddenly, by chance. For the sake of the example, use this one sentence to communicate three possible reactions:

"How wonderful to see you; did you know I'd be here?"

Applying the defense postures suggested above, here are two possible sequences of psycho-physical events.

First sequence
1. At the sight of former lover, adrenalin rushes into the blood, knees go weak, breathing and heart pump faster.
2. Thinks: "I can't let him/her see how much I'm affected."
3. Method: Add social energy to make it a slightly exaggerated and inappropriately extroverted joy which activates the muscles in the throat and face more vigorously than the breath.
4. Result: Channel muscles drive the sound into the nose creating a high pitch of delight which smothers the initial vulnerability in social noise:

"How WON-derful to SEE you: did you KNOW I was HERE?"

(Exaggerated surprise and delight: The question safely assumes the answer "yes.")

Second sequence
1. At the sight of former lover, adrenalin rushes into the blood, knees go weak, breathing and heart pump faster.
2. Thinks: "I wonder if he/she feels the same as I do. Until I know I daren't express what I feel too clearly or I might get hurt."
3. Method: Let out all the breath in a rush while holding the feeling in. Empty breath floods the vocal folds left flaccid by the withheld emotional impulse, creating half-voice, half-whisper that lacks the vibrating energy to stimulate resonating feedback, or lively inflection.
4. Result: half-whispers "How wonderful to see you. Did you know I'd be here."
(Monotone throws the responsibility on to the hearer to project what he or she wants to believe he or she has heard into the unrevealing sentence, thus showing his or her hand first.)

Third sequence
In the event of an open revelation of feeling the psycho-physical sequence could be:

1. At the sight of former lover, adrenalin rushes into the blood, knees go weak, breathing and heart pump faster.

2. The excitement energizes laryngeal musculature governing the vocal folds so that excited breath/excited folds create high frequency vibrations that are picked up and amplified by simultaneously toned-up muscle tissue in the upper pharynx and upper facial areas.

3. Pitch jumps: Light, high resonating quality responds and ex-lover hears the surprised, half-fearful delight and the genuine need to know whether he/she chose to seek him/her out or came here by chance.

STEP 5 ■ *Repeat Steps 1 and 2 fully, with a consciousness of filling in the part of the range that goes from middle to high.*

Start with the "mee-mee-mee"'s, go on to "mey-mey-mey" but release the sound this time into your mouth on "my-my-my-my."

Repeat, and end on one long "my-y-y-y-" on an upward inflection as though for an ingenuous question

$$\text{mee-mee-mee}_{\text{mey-meY-mEY}}{}_{\text{MY-Y-Y-Y-Y-Y?}}$$

Try not to go into falsetto.

Check that your eyebrows don't go up immediately at the idea of a question. If they do go up, your voice won't go as far as it might. (The eyebrows tend to substitute for the soft palate.)

■ *Repeat; and at the end of the questioning "my-y-y?" say "why?" on the same breath, in the same resonance, on the same rising pitch.*

$$\text{meemeemeemeymeYmEYmy}_{YY}{}^{YY\text{WHY}^{YY}}\ ?$$

Spread the "why-y-y?" across your cheekbones.

Repeat "meemeemeemeymeymeymy? why?" and then add

"why fly?" (breath) "why fly so high?"

with the accumulated energy of the pitch, the resonator, the question and an urgency of need to know the answer.

STEP 6 ■ *Imagine you are standing on top of a mountain. There is a narrow deep gulley between it and another peak. The sky is blue, the air is clear and crisp. On the other peak stands a friend of yours.*

Let the scene affect your inner state. From an exhilarated center call a long, high, curving "hi-i-i" across to the opposite mountain peak.

■ *The same scene exactly. Same feelings. Same desire to call. This time whisper the call — just the impulse from center and breath flying out through the wide channel of your throat. A whispered "hi-i-i-i."*

Voice it again.

Here you are providing yourself with the kind of scene that can stimulate the energy that needs the upper to high part of the vocal range and resonating ladder in order to express itself satisfactorily. All the technical work must be trusted to pay off automatically. The calling impulse should travel naturally to the diaphragm without being subverted by the throat muscles; the diaphragm should spontaneously draw in enough breath to supply that impulse and willingly release the breath and impulse with energy sufficient for the demand. By now the throat, the soft palate and the jaw should be naturally limber and agile enough to fly out of the way of the call, which will be impelled into high, carrying resonators capable of amplifying the vibrations enough to accomplish the goal of communicating with your friend on the opposite mountain peak.

It is important now that you begin to create your own simple scenes so that you can alternate between the technical, conscious work that will develop a tuned-up, toned-up, fit vocal instrument, and the imaginative work that knows the voice must function involuntarily if it is to be true. In the technical work you carve out paths from the mind to chosen muscles; in the imaginative work you know those paths are there and you run along them. You are reconditioning your use of yourself, not just something called "your voice," so when you follow a scene, feed the *initial* impulse of image to the place where the path begins before you start. Start from the center, feed the center, release from the center and see what happens. If you stumble or fall, go back to do a bit more carving in the technical department. Then deliver yourself up again to your creative self. From technical to creative and back again, but at this stage, do not try to combine the two or your energies will split and lose their strength.

12: Range

Within the framework of the resonating ladder, only the domed top of the head remains to be explored. The top of the resonating ladder has a perfect acoustical shape and texture. It resounds simply and strongly to the high frequency sounds that find amplification there, but unless you are a practicing soprano, tenor, counter-tenor or scream daily, you may not be familiar with the feeling of skull resonance. There is intense energy in the sound which must be created centrally if it is to serve some human purpose, and it is easier to lead into the exercises for developing skull resonance from simple work on the whole range (which will allow such energy to generate naturally), than to make a direct assault on it. In theory, the work on the skull goes before that on range, but in practice it is more helpful to work on the range exercises first. In the following exercises you will be using your developing awareness of a resonating ladder to free your voice into its widest possible range.

STEP 1 ▪ *Standing easily with awareness of the skeletal support of your body, close your eyes and turn your attention inward.*
Imagine your body is a house. Put the basement below the rib cage, the ground floor in the chest, the first floor in the mouth, second floor from the mouth to the eyes, third floor from the eyebrows to the hairline, and the attic in the top of the skull.

▪ *Picture your voice as an elevator whose electrical mechanism is* in the basement, and using a long "he-e-ey" as the sound in which your voice/elevator is manifested, travel from basement to attic visiting all the resonating floors on the way.

Take into account the fact that a house does not move when the elevator has to run, (let your mouth drop open, but otherwise do not allow your shoulders, jaw, tongue, lips or eyebrows to help in any way by moving as the voice/elevator moves).

■ Let the breath replace after you have arrived in the attic, and, renewing the electrical power from the basement, travel down through the house again, making sure you do not skip any of the floors and that the elevator runs at the same smooth pace all the way down. (There is a tendency to skid out of control on the way down, jumping from attic to first floor and spending a great deal of time on the ground floor.)

Imagine your body
is a house.

■ Repeat the exercise several times until you are familiar with the idea.

Points to look out for are:

The power that moves the elevator comes from the basement, whether starting from the basement or the attic.

If you feel you are running out of that power halfway up or down, don't squeeze the last volt out, get a fresh boost from below. This is not an exercise to test how long you can sustain one breath.

Let your attention be on the accuracy of the image and the sensory perception of resonance; let pitch be a by-product of these.

STEP 2 Having visited thus the resonating chambers of your body, now deal with the range carelessly and freely.

■ *Drop down the spine very quickly and build up as quickly. The* drop down goes in two unequal stages: a sudden, heavy drop of the head, and a quick undoing of the spine. (Make sure your knees bend as you do this or you will be thrown off balance.) The build-up starts as a rebound from the sudden drop, goes fast up the spine, the head floating up also.

■ Start the "hey" at the bottom of your range in your stomach, drop your head and begin to go up your range as you drop down the spine. Let the ascending pitch and the descending spine accelerate so that the sudden, bumpy drop at the bottom expels the top part of the range out through the top of your head very freely. New breath. Start the "hey" at the top of your range. Build up your spine as the sound travels down the range, arriving back in your stomach by the time your head floats back up on top of the spine.

■ Go up the range as you go down the spine, and down the range as you go up the spine with the following awarenesses:

Mentally take advantage of gravity to allow the top of your range to go higher in pitch each time you drop down. Think of the sound as falling upward out of your skull.

Be loose, free, careless; the bump as you suddenly drop down should shock the sound upward.

Don't hold on to the top note — let it swoop out giddily.

Don't adopt too serious an attitude to the exercise or you will destroy its purpose.

A useful picture to play with is, when you are standing the "hey" starts in your tailbone and travels up your spine to your head where it escapes through a hole in the top. When you are upside-down it starts under the ground then flows from your head down to the tailbone again by the time you are upright.

STEP 3   ■ Lie on your back on the floor and travel slowly through the range, examining and relishing all the rungs of the resonating ladder. Again, the spinal picture can be useful: This time, while supine, think of the spine as a railroad track and the sound as a train traveling from the tailbone depot to the topmost vertebra terminal and vice-versa.

In this position you can really check that you are moving through the whole range of your voice using only your mind and your breath. You do not need to open your mouth wider as you go higher or lower, you do not need to push with your throat muscles to reach the high notes, you do not need to press your head back or lift your eyebrows. Thought and breath are all you need.

STEP 4   ■ Stand up and repeat Steps 1 and 2 with the awareness of Step 3.

13: The skull resonators

Step 1 of this chapter will link the range-freeing process with skull exploration exercises. I am going to introduce a concept here which can be very useful if grasped clearly. In Step 2 of the previous chapter the physical process of suddenly dropping your body upside down propelled the sound upward without obvious muscular effort. All your abdominal muscles should have felt totally relaxed at that point, so you do not need much extra muscle power to support a high sound. Yet extra energy has to be generated. Try that step again when you are upright: Repeat the sounds immediately, standing still, and consciously transfer the physical energy into mental energy.

The physical energy generated by a body dropping through space in response to gravity is great. The mind can use the experience of such release to generate mental energy that is as great, if not greater, than the physical energy.

This means that high sounds can be produced with very little extra work in observable muscles. High notes are produced through increased aerodynamic pressure between the breath and the vocal folds created with greater tension in the breathing musculature and the laryngeal musculature. The danger is that that knowledge *adds* still more tension in the form of conscious abdominal support, thus spoiling a delicate balance of energies understandable only on the involuntary level of neuro-physical response. Economy of effort is essential to truthful results. To put it another way, as soon as the abdominal muscles pull in, push out or do something conscious to boost the sound, they substitute physical energy for mental energy. Mental energy, in the case of the high part of the voice, usually implies emotional energy so the substitution is crucial.

STEP 1   ■ *Drop quickly down the spine going up through the range on "hey." Register the topmost sound that flies out through the attic when you are upside down: It should by now be a high falsetto sound for both men and women. Allow a new breath and, still upside down, release a high, falsetto "keeee" on the same pitch as your voice fell into in the attic. (The "keeee" can be something like a yodel, and should not be sustained on one note for too long.)*

Relax, and slowly build up the spine. When you are upright yodel out the high falsetto "keeee" again. You should feel it ring into the dome of the skull.

A useful pattern of sound for this is:

Keee - eee   ∅   Keee - eee   ∅   Keee - ∅ eee

Men should start a little lower but most can go as high as the above suggested pitches.

As a variation and for greater flexibility think the following pattern as a quick, light oscillation in the falsetto release:

Keee - ee - ee - ee - eee - eee   ∅ Keee - ee - ee - ee - ee - eee

In response to the lively mental energy needed to create these sounds a lively breath response from center will be felt. Let that happen but try not to add any extra pull from the *external* abdominal wall muscles. The abdominal wall will move, but passively, pulled from inside as the diaphragm moves up, *not* because it must actively push the breath out. It is necessary to know the difference between a strong physical movement that is active on the voluntary, neuro-muscular level, and a strong physical movement that is reactive on the involuntary level. The muscles should respond from inside the body and because everything is connected, the outside will move too. The internal breathing musculature is stimulated by powerful impulses into powerful activity, and the energy thus generated is of a different quality from that produced by effort in the large external muscles.

STEP 2 ■ *Inject the powerful impulse of the thought of a high, falsetto "keeee-eee" such as you produced in Step 1, but this time whisper it. The strong thought impulse will arouse a strong response from the center of the diaphragm releasing a strong breath hissing through the front teeth.*

■ *Whisper "keeee-eee" several times, concentrating on reproducing the thought of the falsetto pitch and allowing the body to react to that thought with appropriate energy. New thought impulse, new breath impulse each time.*

■ *Then voice it, dealing with thought, breath and inner energy and letting the sound be a by-product of them.*

■ *Repeat on ascending pitches, alternating the whispered and the voiced "keeee-eee" 's.*

When you do this fully you are conditioning the dedication of communicative energy to cause.

STEP 3 ■ *Drop your voice down to the bottom of your range and with the relaxation of your mind and your breath rumble sound deep into your chest resonance on "hey."*

You may find that the resultant sound is much deeper than before as the vocal folds relax more fully after their unaccustomed stretching.

STEP 4 ■ *Experiment with calling, on "hey," as high as you can go without slipping into falsetto. Men, particularly, can find a strong, ringing sound that has an intense existence in the top of the dome of the skull and is easy to maintain there once it is free of the throat and connected to appropriately strong energy from the center.*

Women should experiment with the high, falsetto "keee-eee" extending their range into a mouselike squeak. Do this lightly and playfully — swooping the sounds, never holding onto the last or first note, letting the energy spring as though from a jack-in-the-box from center.

The first objective in working to free the very top of the range is to remove doubts, fears and unfamiliarity. The quality of the sound is irrelevant, although as the vocal folds strengthen and the throat frees you develop excellent raw material for a soprano or tenor voice and rich counter-tenor quality. But beauty must wait until freedom is assured.

Falsetto work increases the elasticity and strength of the vocal folds and the breathing muscles. (This part of the range can be referred to as the "loft register.") It is useful for both men's and women's voices because the whole range will benefit from such strengthening if it is done as the final part of a well-balanced workout on the voice. Men are no longer as culturally averse to experimenting with the falsetto part of their voices as they used to be, although some still make a subconscious protest at its unmanliness by being unable to find it. Similarly, many women still seem to feel subconsciously that chest resonance is not for them, preferring the "feminine" appeal of their upper register. A man can compete easily with a woman's soprano range and develop at least two octaves in a falsetto that is mellow and unforced. For both men and women, work in the high, falsetto, skull-resonating area develops flexibility and strength in the rest of the voice. It also removes inhibitions, releases powerful energies and provides a familiarity with intense vibrations of feeling and sound. This allows the expression of emotional extremes with ease and excitement, without trauma and without straining the voice.

As with all the exercises suggested so far, these top of the skull sounds should be done in context and their context is the top of the resonating ladder. You should not plunge into any of the high sounds until you have thoroughly limbered up the voice. I strongly recommend that you develop a sequence of exercises that takes you from conscientious physical relaxation through all the steps taken from Chapter 3 to 13 *and in that progression*. Do not alter the sequence or make arbitrary jumps within it until you are quite sure of what you are doing. In the beginning it may seem unorganic. Your body and your voice may seem to tell you that you don't need such-and-such an exercise whereas this other one is essential. Unfortunately your "instinct" may be some ingrained, crafty habit fighting to maintain your vocal status quo; if you doggedly persist in doing the most unpopular exercises along with the others you will be covering *every* aspect of the whole regularly. It is easy to become enamoured of your chest resonance, your mask resonance, even your falsetto, and if you give any one area more time than other less-favored areas, you will end up with as unbalanced and inflexible a voice as had been dictated previously by habit.

Part three:
Sensitivity and power

14: Breathing power

Up to this point it has deliberately been implied by omission that the diaphragm is the only muscle that need be considered as far as breathing is concerned. It has been pointed out that there is no convenient space underneath the diaphragm so that when you breathe in and the diaphragm descends, the stomach is pushed down and the intestines are moved around to make room. Consequently the stomach area must stay relaxed so as not to inhibit the ingoing breath. It is convenient to imagine that the breath itself goes down into the belly so that two mental processes can become one. Although the direct effect of this imaginary device is the relaxation of inhibitory contractions in the lower abdomen, it indirectly stimulates the internal abdominal breathing musculature which, attached from the fourth lumbar vertebra to the diaphragm itself, pulls it down, flattening it as part of the process that draws air into the lungs.

I have laid heavy emphasis on relaxation in the realm of breathing. It takes so long for such deep relaxation to become familiar and for organic awareness to develop as a result, that it is wise to postpone work that increases breathing capacity and strengthens the breathing musculature until it can be done with awareness and sensitivity to ensure that breath stays in touch with inner energy impulse whatever the demand. A larger breath capacity and more powerful breathing muscles should imply a larger emotional capacity and a more powerful desire to communicate. Otherwise you develop sound and fury which signify nothing. Large lung capacity per se is almost irrelevant to the problem of whether a breath lasts through a sentence. For instance, the capacity developed in underwater swimming does not serve the needs of an emotionally long-winded speech.

Any attempt to sustain breath by holding it back or preserving it sets up tensions that defeat the objective. This is why the old-fashioned exercises in "rib reserve" are so counter-productive. The effort involved in holding the ribs open for as long as possible, in order to maintain a reserve tank of air, inevitably creates tension that contracts the natural capacity. The intercostal breathing muscles expand and contract in the involuntary rhythm of natural breathing. If they are interfered with and asked to perform such an unnatural task as holding the rib cage open, there is severe dislocation in the deep, instinctual connection between emotion and breath. If you are holding muscularly you are holding mentally. Elasticity in the breathing muscles is essential to mental agility, and strength must not be acquired at the expense of subtlety. Strength however, must be acquired.

We will now be moving carefully into a phase of exercise which will test all your awareness of mind-body unity if it is to pay off in the interest of greater expression, not just greater noise.

There are three sets of breathing muscles that make up the whole apparatus: Abdominal, diaphragmatic and intercostal. The "costae" are the ribs; the "intercostals" are the muscles that are in between the rib bones and it is to these that we will now apply the stretching and relaxing process; first to make them elastic and flexible, then to make them longer so that they create a larger cavity inside which the lungs can expand further. It is important that you are now capable of sending specific messages to stimulate activity in the rib muscles isolated from the stomach muscles. Work on one part of the breathing apparatus can have an unnoticed negative effect on another, so that gain in one area is offset by loss in the other.

You may, in the previous total attention given to the diaphragm and abdominal breathing, have allowed the ribs to give in to the nether regions. You may even have become quite sunken in the chest as you focused more and more on the satisfactory depths of the lower stomach. Without losing that deep access it is now time to add some upper expansion.

One of the duties of the intercostal muscles is to lift the sheer weight of the rib bones off the lungs. Imagine for the moment the weight of bone in the twenty-four ribs that make up the rib cage, and imagine that weight lying on two sponges. The lungs are roughly in the state of the two sponges when the intercostals are not doing their job. The upper part of the spine is, of course, the most vital element in supporting the rib cage. The intercostal support is secondary. If the section of the spine that runs up between the shoulder blades is weak, this will have one of two results in the posture of the rib cage. Either the upper chest will hollow and the lower ribs will disappear as the spine droops, or the rib muscles will take over the job of supporting the chest. The latter response deploys the strength of the intercostals posturally to such a degree that there is nothing left with which to pump the lungs.

Bear in mind that the layer of intercostal muscles that directly pump the spongy lungs is on the *inside* walls of the rib cage as you proceed slowly through the following exercises. These demand more powerful mental pictures in order to stimulate more powerful movements; it is only through the imagination that you can exercise the involuntary musculature deliberately.

STEP 1
Rib awareness

• *Stand and begin an arm stretch to the ceiling, paying particular attention to your back. Feel that the back is pulled away from the spine as the elbows move forward and then upward. Picture the back being stretched first horizontally and then on an upgoing diagonal.*

Let the arms be lifted by the muscles in the undersides of the arms, from below. Be aware of the angle made in the armpit between the upper arm and the side ribs; note how the angle widens as the arms go higher.

Observe a connection between the arms and the side ribs which dictates movement in the ribs in response to the arm stretch.

Yawn as your hands stretch to the sky; feel your hands stretch as if yawning; feel the back of your throat stretch; feel your back ribs stretch with the yawn.

Let the wrists go, drop the elbows, arms, head. Now go very slowly down through the section of the spine between the shoulder blades. It is not as easy to make specific contact with the vertebrae here as it is in the small of the back or the back of the neck, but if you picturn the skeletal structure very clearly and allow the rib cage to crumble as you take each vertbra away, you can sense the relationship of ribs to spine.

When you are hanging head downward put your hands on your middle back and sigh deeply feeling the response in the back ribs. In this position it should be easy to feel the breath going into your back — a sensation that gets neglected when standing upright.

Build up the spine, keeping a mental picture of the breadth and mobility of your back.

There is, of course, more mobility in the sides and front of the rib cage because of the floating ribs, but they will take care of themselves if the back is released. The side ribs sometimes take over too much responsibility in the breathing process. They pump very efficiently but at the expense of the sensitivity of the delicate diaphragm/solar plexus connection.

STEP 2
Rib stretching ■ *Standing, feel with your fingertips the bottom edge of your rib cage from the breast-bone around to the spine. Dig your fingers firmly enough into the bottom of the back ribs to leave a clear impression as to their location.*

Imagine that there is a short, strong piece of elastic attaching your lower back ribs to your elbow points.

Lift the elbows a little, straight up and out from the sides, and feel the back ribs respond as the imagined elastic pulls. Establish that powerful mental connection between the elbows and the lower back ribs. Let the elbows drop.

Lift the elbows up from your sides again, this time taking them right up until they are on a level with your shoulders. This should have the effect of pulling your back and side ribs well up and out from the spine so that the entire back of the rib cage gets stretched.

Now take your elbows forward in a wide arc and stretch your back even more.

Bring the elbows back, allowing the back intercostals to relax a little.

Move the elbows forward to stretch the back intercostals.

Bring them back to relax the intercostals.

Lower the arms home to your sides and let the back intercostals relax completely.

■ *Now apply the same process to the front of the rib cage to stretch and relax the front intercostal muscles.*

Imagine the short, strong elastic attachment from elbows to the bottom of the front of the rib cage.

Float the arms up to shoulder height, pulling the bottom of the rib cage out to the sides with the emphasis on the front and floating ribs.

Move the elbows back a little, to stretch the front of the rib cage more.

Bring the elbows forward again to relax the intercostals.

Stretch; relax.

Lower the arms down to your sides, letting the front intercostals relax totally.

■ *Float the elbows up to shoulder height.*

Move them forward pulling the back of the rib cage wide open.

Keep the back of the rib cage as it is and move the elbows back pulling the front of the rib cage open.

You should now have a rather uncomfortably expanded barrel chest.

■ *Wriggle the rib cage up and even wider until you can picture it as an opened umbrella.*

Keeping the rib cage where it is, lower your arms and relax your shoulders. (You should still be in a grotesque position with your ribs overexpanded, high and stretched, making it hard to breathe.) Now think of releasing the front ribs enough to allow you to breathe easily, but keep the spine long and don't let your back ribs collapse. Then let the whole rib cage collapse as though you were dropping your rib bones into your stomach.

■ *Repeat the whole sequence without the final collapse. There will be a tendency to pull forward and up in the shoulders which must be vigorously counteracted by increasing the focus of the mind on the lower part of the rib cage. The shoulders should stay relaxed throughout; the stretch runs from the bottom of the rib cage up the sides and along the underside of the upper arms to the elbows — a lateral stretch.*

Make sure you do not arch the small of the back as you stretch. A good check on this is to keep your knees a little bent. Locked knees and an over-arched lower spine nearly always go together.

If you can stretch and relax the intercostal muscles independently of breath, so much the better. You will tend to breathe in as you open the rib cage, back or front, and breathe out as you relax it. But if you can make direct contact with the actual muscles through your image of the structure you will exercise them apart from habitual breathing patterns. Once reunited, the breath will find new spaces, more variety and a chance to alter patterns.

Awareness of the breathing apparatus as a six-sided box

■ *Lie on the floor on your front, face to the floor, forehead on hands. Take advantage of the immobilization of your most flexible breathing area (stomach, floating ribs on the inflexible floor,) to discover possibilities for breathing in your back.*
Sigh deeply down into the bottom of your spine. Imagine you have lungs in your buttocks. Let the air fill you from your buttocks, through the small of your back to your back ribs. Let it escape in the same order.

■ *Roll over onto your back and picture your torso as a rectangular box with six sides: (1) your back from the nape of the neck to the tailbone; (2) your front from the collar-bone to the pubic bone; (3) and (4) your two sides from armpit to hip-joint; (5) your shoulder girdle; (6) your pelvic girdle. Imagine that the box is made of an elastic material so that it can be moved from inside in every direction.*

■ *Feed a deep sigh of relief into the six-sided elastic box so that the breath/relief moves:*
> *your pelvis toward your feet*
> *your back into the floor*
> *your front toward the ceiling*
> *your sides out laterally*
> *your shoulder girdle toward your head*
Then let the breath/relief fall out of you, uncontrolled, with the inside elastic walls of the six-sided box collapsing inward toward each other.

■ *Roll onto your right side, immobilizing it by the floor contact. Sigh into your left side.*
Roll onto your left side immobilizing it. Sigh into your right side.
Roll onto your back and sigh into the whole six-sided apparatus, registering the availability of your torso for the large breath.

STEP 4 ■ *Stand up. Observe your ordinary, everyday, natural breathing rhythm (a small exchange of easy breaths) in terms of the six-sided box. It is as useful for small breaths as it is for large ones; only the movements are infinitely subtler.*

■ *Feed in gradually increasing sighs of relief in this upright position. Use your observation of the back, the lower spine, and the sides, while you were on the floor, to help make more space avail-*

126   Sensitivity and power

able now that you are standing. Pay particular attention to the connection of breathing to the pelvic floor.

■ *Use the concept of the six-sided box as a new basis of awareness for a full workout on your voice.*

To stimulate an extended use of the breathing box within the framework of familiar exercises, enlarge your image of where the sound is traveling to, increase your indulgence in the sound, boost your need to speak. That is, move the person to whom you are speaking or calling further away; lengthen the sentence or take longer to say it. For instance, instead of "haa-haa-haa huh-huh-huh hee-hee-hee," think: "haaaa-haaaa-haaaa-haaaa-haaaa," lovingly wallow in the rumbles in your chest: / "huh-huh-huh-huh-huh-huh," bounce the sounds briskly round your mouth: / "hee-hee-hee-hee-hee-hee," sharply drill your teeth with the vibrations.

Play with the idea of increasing inner impulse in order to extend muscular exercise as imaginatively as you can.

The image of the elastic six-sided box is intended to help create a sense of immense inner spaciousness. The breathing capacity must be enlarged to serve larger emotions. We often respond to larger emotions with greater effort, particularly when acting, and greater effort means muscular tension, which means contraction, which means a smaller capacity. This is self-defeating. If the whole of the inside of the torso can be continued to greet a large emotional impulse with a welcoming expansion, we are halfway toward being able to communicate that emotion freely.

When you sigh with the profound relief designed to expand the whole six-sided box, picture the relief going down to the pelvic floor first and then filling you up like water filling up a jug, from the bottom up. This is not so much to make a rule about the order in which the breathing muscles should respond, but to make sure that no area is left out.

It is sometimes a revelation to realize that there are breathing connections all the way down into the groin. Yet if you sit in a chair, really relax your stomach and buttocks and cough you will feel a movement in the anal sphincters. The phrase "tight-assed" uses an accurate physiological phenomenon to convey a psychological one. When you respond to an emotional condition with tension you will probably not only be tight in the stomach but also rigid in the lower spine and squeezed in the sphincters. There is no way in which energy can flow freely in such a state.

The next exercise is designed to stimulate the whole breathing apparatus as vigorously as possible using strong involuntary reflexes. It is called "vacuuming the lungs": Partly because there is a sense of cleaning them out, but mainly because it uses the natural power of a vacuum to stimulate the breathing muscles into powerful action.

The exercise takes a very short time to do but a long time to explain, so read all the instructions first, then follow the quick step-by-step action.

Explanation You are going to empty all the air out of your lungs as though you were squeezing water out of a sponge. You will do this by blowing out (on "fffff") quickly and then squeezing the last remnants of air out until you feel there is no more inside you. (Don't take too long over this). Quickly close your mouth and pinch your nose shut with your fingers so that no air can get in. Now open up your rib cage creating the image of a large vacuum inside. The best way of doing this is to try to breathe in through the nose, still pinched shut, and allow the intercostal muscles to respond to the demand by expanding the chest cavity despite the fact that no breath can get in. Register the pull of the vacuum for a moment. Then, *keeping your mouth closed*, let go of your nose. Air will rush in through your nose to fill the vacuum. Don't help by breathing in. Let the breath be sucked in by the law of nature that abhors a vacuum.

Action ■ *Stand.*

Empty your lungs on "fffffff."

Hold your nose; close your mouth.

Try to breathe in so that your ribs expand as far as they can (the open umbrella position.)

Picture the vacuum you have created.

. . . *vacuuming the lungs*

Let go of your nose, keeping the mouth shut, and let the air rush in to fill the vacuum.
Return to natural breathing.

Some people have a moment's panic when they feel the vacuum. It is, after all, a very unnatural condition. But remember that it would only be dangerous to be without air if the condition were controlled by anyone else but you. All you have to do is open your mouth and things will return to normal. Once you have become familiar with the general format you can extend your awareness while you experience it.

Action with
picture: ■ *Think of your lungs as filling the whole torso and do the vacuuming with the picture of the six-sided box.*
Blow all the air out of your body. Feel all the elastic walls of the six-sided box move toward each other.
Hold your nose; close your mouth.
Expand the six-sided box in all directions to create a vacuum through your whole torso.
Let go of your nose and feel the air rush down to the pelvic floor, into your sides, your back and your front.
Relax and return to natural breathing.

You will probably be dizzy with all that extra oxygen rushing in. If you are not it could be a sign that you are not doing the exercise fully. It could also mean that your breathing apparatus is in good shape already. Don't be afraid of the dizziness, but don't overdo it by repeating the vacuuming over and over too quickly. Rest, do other exercises and then come back to it. As you exercise your breathing apparatus the dizziness will disappear.

Vacuuming the lungs fits into a vocal warm-up just after the chest and mouth resonator work. It limbers up the energies before going on to the middle and upper part of the range. Vacuum three or four times, sometimes slowly, sometimes fast. It invigorates the whole system and is a generally healthy exercise, but its main purpose at the moment is to strengthen the breathing muscles by the use of natural reflexive movements. If you practice "deep breathing" exercises to achieve strength, you build muscular control which will not serve spontaneous communication. The importance of maintaining the relationship between impulse and muscular activity cannot be over-emphasized as we move into the more vigorous exercises which are necessary if the vocal apparatus and the emotional apparatus of an actor are to develop simultaneously. If the voice develops independent strength, it can substitute sound for feeling and there is nothing more insidiously corrosive to an actor's artistry than the consciousness of growing vocal energies which are more accessible than emotional energies. Conversely, the actor may be developing the emotional instrument faster than the vocal one, and the resulting short circuit can blow all the fuses in the house. It is idealistic to suggest that an actor can maintain a strict balance while working on body, voice and creativity, but if the aim is idealistic at least there is the possibility of some quality along the way.

Actors who have "good voices" and have been complimented on them are sometimes surprised, if not offended, when I commiserate with them on their gift. It is nearly always those actors who have the greatest trouble finding their emotional resources. Those who start with weak vocal instruments tend to be better off in the long run as dependence on the inner life pays off and the voice gradually learns to serve it freely.

In the next exercise you will be integrating the general picture of the six-sided breathing box with the intercostals and the diaphragm. The larger capacity found in the total picture must incorporate growing flexibility if sensitivity is not to be sacrificed to power. Therefore the next point of attention will once again be the diaphragm.

STEP 5   Prepare for this by stretching, relaxing, rolling the head and so on. The success of this exercise depends on your ability to start with your body in a neutral state so that you can genuinely work from impulse and allow things to *happen to* the body.

▪ *You are going to feed four huge impulses for sighs of relief— genuine, deeply felt, pleasurable relief— into the six-sided breathing box, one immediately after the other. Don't hurry them, but don't wait in between.*

Let the impulse move the breath and let the breath move the body. (Treat the pleasurable relief as though it were an acting exercise if necessary. Think of something bad that was about to happen but didn't, leaving you with a huge sense of relief. If you program this once or twice you should then be able to go directly to the sigh without it being merely a big breath with no content.)

Do four huge sighs in a row and then rest. (If you do more you court fainting.)

In a mental picture of the process, the diaphragm, as a trampoline-like shelf dissecting the breathing box, should appear to be blown up and down by the gale of wind raised by the impulses. Your insides will be quite discombobulated by the disturbance if the sighs are gusty enough. The external abdominal wall must be like jelly, being moved quite violently by the inner turbulence but not actively controlling it.

Repeat the four big sighs of relief.

Rest.

■ You are now going to feed in six repeated impulses for sighs of relief. This time, however, they will be slightly smaller, faster and affect you more toward the center of the dome of the diaphragm. Only on the very last one will the whole breathing box collapse with a final deep yielding to the relief pouring out.

This will now seem rather like panting; it is, but do not take the short cut of calling it panting. Program the impulse connection conscientiously until you can be confident that the muscle movement will trigger the impulse as surely as impulse triggers the muscles. Then you can work from the inside out or the outside in safely.

Exercise your ability to recreate repeated impulses of relief without becoming shallow, thoughtless or mechanical.

Repeat the four huge, turbulent sighs.

Repeat the six smaller, faster sighs confined more to the diaphragm area.

■ Focus your attention on the very center of the dome of the diaphragm and feed in many quick, lively impulses to flutter the breath in and out on that center. Let the feeling behind the impulses change to pleasurable anticipation, capable of delivering faster stimuli than relief. Let the anticipation stimulate the breath and let the breath flutter the center of the dome of the diaphragm, so that the breath flies in and out fast and loose and then releases in a final sigh of relief.

Leave the outside muscles of the torso really loose; they will be moved but should not get tight at any point. The breath goes in and out evenly; that is, you should not get fuller as you go on nor should your lungs empty in the course of the exercise. In theory you should be able to continue for a long time with the breath going in and out this quickly, because as much goes in as out each time. In fact, the muscles will get tighter as you go faster, so do the exercise in short sequences.

The exercise therefore is this: Ten or so quick, light anticipation impulses, then release on relief; anticipation — relief — anticipation — relief. The quicker, the lighter, the more central, the better.

In the first part of this exercise the repetition of four big sighs of relief is intended to accustom the whole breathing capacity to supplying a large demand quickly, and to release quickly without controlling. In the second part more energy is generated and the agility of the breathing muscles is tested. In the third part the agility increases, flexibility is essential and an important reconditioning process is introduced: to remain free of tension while the intensity of emotional energy increases. This, of course, is using the word "tension" with the common meaning of "holding." Emotional energy stimulates a great deal of activity in the muscles and the conditioning you must do allows the energy to flow refusing to let any muscle clutch, hold or stop the energy flow.

It is often necessary to remind an actor not to hold on to an emotional condition. It feels so good when the feeling suddenly comes that the actor wants to nurse it, yet in doing so it dies. If the actor has the courage to spend feeling freely at such a moment, more feeling will be naturally generated. Muscles that hold onto feeling kill it, but muscles that are conductors of that feeling help propagate more feeling through the mutuality of neuro-muscular function.

The panting exercises, if done with true mind/body unity, not only make the breathing musculature fit enough to serve the emotional instrument but also can be used to stimulate pure energy when you are physically lethargic and unreceptive to inner stimuli.

You may by now be questioning the repetition of the sigh. Sighs of relief, pleasurable relief, now become *pleasurable* anticipation. This choice as a means of stimulating the breath is made because it is easier to learn to respond to increasing energy and intensity dealing with positive, optimistic content rather than one that is unpleasant. The deconditioning of protective muscle reaction and the reconditioning of giving and receiving energy without inhibition can happen faster under pleasurable circumstances. Eventually, however, this reconditioning must pay off in the interest of an exchange of human experience that includes fear, pain, misery, anger, panic, depression, doubt, hate, etc. Usually it is best to deal with these emotions in the context of a speech or scene, having established the format of freedom in more positive feelings. It would be irresponsible to offer in a book means by which the reader could tap and release powerful emotions of a non-positive nature. In the laboratory atmosphere of a classroom or studio, fears can be allayed by common experience and emotional energy can be channeled into the context of the actor's needs. All emotions can be labelled positive as familiarity creates a natural control. But working on self in these areas is difficult because there has to be a moment at which you lose control and someone trustworthy must be there to make use of that moment, channeling the new energy into the work at hand. Otherwise it can be emotional masturbation and/or a blind freakout.

The answer to this problem is not that it all belongs in acting class or therapy, but in accepting that voice work must be acting work and vice versa.

Here is a relatively light-hearted story which can be used with the panting exercise to illustrate ways in which you can safely inject some variety of content into any exercise. If you can get someone to tell it to you step by step, so much the better. Otherwise practice being able to visualize a sequence of events specifically and without anticipation, even though you know the story.

Preamble: This morning in the mail you received an anonymous note telling you that this evening at five o'clock, you should take the nearest train (or bus or subway) to a particular station just outside the city (or town). There you were to go out of the station, turn left and go down to the end of the road where there would be a large house set back from the road in its own garden. You were instructed that the house would be empty, the door unlocked, and you were to go in, up the stairs, down the long corridor on the left, and into the room at the end where you were to wait.

All this you have done.

You are now waiting in an empty room, in an empty house and dusk is gathering.

The exercise: Let us assume that you are in a state of anticipation. Let the anticipation stimulate your breathing quite arbitrarily into a loose panting rhythm such as you have just explored. Feed everything that happens from now on directly into the panting center.

You are standing in the middle of the room, listening. Suddenly, downstairs, you hear the front door open and close. / Hear this with your breathing.

You hear footsteps going slowly across the hall below. / Let it affect the breathing in the center—don't let the muscles tighten—just let the breathing quicken.

The steps come slowly up the stairs and start down the corridor. / The panting should quicken—still centered. / Leave the outside muscles loose.

The steps come slowly closer and closer to your room and stop outside the door. / Very fast, free panting.

The door opens and it's your favorite friend. / Release the breath on a great pleasurable sigh of relief.

Trying not to be critical of such a simple-minded story, make use of the atmospheric elements to introduce sensory provocation to a place in your body where it can arouse feelings which intensify and finally go through a transition in response to a new sensory provocation. The panting forbids the muscular contractions that inhibit productive reaction at various stages along the road, and ensures that breath is constantly leaving the body carrying the feeling on it. This is spontaneous communication.

Be sure you really feel the emotional transit from anticipation to relief when you see your friend. (There are various reactions you may have, of course, to such a scene. React as you will but let it be on panting and a sigh, with a transition between the two.)

The big point here is to decondition a neuro-muscular process that produces tension in response to intensity, and to recondition the neuro-muscular response to one of release. In other words, to be able to develop mental intensity without physical tension.

STEP 6 ■ *Practice the quick, central, anticipation breathing on sound.*

Imagine that the diaphragm is a trampoline slung from the bottom edges of the rib cage.

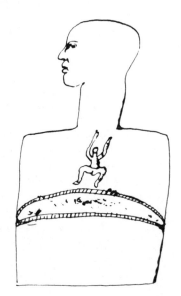

Picture the sound as a little person bouncing up and down in the middle of the trampoline. (The breath goes in between each "huh" sound, however fast the person bounces.)

Bounce he/she 6 or 7 times, then let the person on the trampoline take a flying leap out of your mouth and across the room

      huh Ø huh Ø huh Ø huh
      Ø huh Ø huh Ø
      hu-u-u-u-uh

STEP 7 ■ *Repeat the lonely house story with sound.*

15: The center

The link between breath and inner energy is forged in sensitivity, and depends on sensitivity for its continuation through the largest expression. If asked to list the essential attributes for an actor's voice, the answer could be: range, variety, beauty, clarity, power, volume; but its sensitivity is the quality that will validate all the others. For these others are dull attributes unless they are reflecting the range of feelings, the variety of the mind, the beauty of the content, the clarity of the imagination, the power of the emotion, the volume of the need to communicate. Energies that fuel the voice muscles need to be attuned with great sensitivity to the still finer energies of psychological creation if the communication from inside to outside is going to be transparently true. When the energy of the content is powerful, the more economically it can be communicated the more truthfully it will be revealed.

The concept of working from inside has been applied from the beginning in this method and therefore economy of effort has been practiced all along. As physical awareness refines, however, more and more subtlety can be used, and the next step will be to find how the working concept of center can be refined to achieve greater economy.

The idea of a central point in the dome of the diaphragm which touches sound was introduced in Chapter 5. Thereafter the word center was used more and more frequently as in feeling-center, breathing-center, energy-center, center of the torso. In this chapter I want to suggest two paradoxical approaches to the center. One is to pin down more precisely where it is, and the other is to say that it can be anywhere.

When center becomes jargon we fall into the trap words make for us of supposing we have experienced something because we remember the word that described that thing. Center means one thing to Martha Graham, another to Michael Chekov and other things to others and to me. It is a practical word, but only if one does not deify it to the point of searching for it as the Holy Grail containing Absolute Truth. The value in general that the word has is that wherever The Center may be placed in the body, the very fact of looking for it, and working from it clears the mind and focuses energy. The state of being improves, and naturally so does the performance of the task at hand. The strict, physiological benefit of centering the voice is that the more economically the breath plays on the vocal folds, the better the tone. Too much breath blows the folds apart producing a "breathy" voice. On the other hand, economy must not mean holding back. The use of a sigh of relief in almost all the breathing exercises up to now has been designed to release the mind from any tendency to hold back. Now, assuming that mental condition has been established, we can look for more economy in the use of the breath without danger of holding back.

At the end of the previous chapter, the fast anticipatory panting was happening in the center of the diaphragm. When you begin to use sound with an awareness of the center of the panting movement, you should find that you use less breath, and that which you do use replaces more easily than before. All the movements producing the sound can diminish while the sound remains as strong as the mind thinks it is.

The next exercise is a mental one to refine further the use of the center, thereby transferring still more of the responsibility for sound-making from the body to the mind.

STEP 1 ■ Let the fast panting on center happen in such a way that you can hear the outgoing and incoming breaths clearly. Take particular note of the incoming breaths as they tend to disappear with speed, indicating that the diaphragm is gathering tension.

■ Now, close your mouth and very lightly induce such a fast version of the panting that it is just a quiver on center and hardly disturbs the breath at all. Then let go.

Quiver—let go—quiver—let go.

(Imagine your rib cage is a bird cage with a hummingbird in it. The speed of the quiver-pant has the quality of the quick flutter of a hummingbird's wings. When you release after the quiver, the bird escapes.)

■ *Open your mouth and do the same quiver. Try it hanging head downward so that the diaphragm is quite relaxed. Retaining that freedom, build up the spine again.*

■ *Touch of sound on that quiver center. A very specific contact.*

Now you are going from that center to an inner center. The exercise will lead you to a place that seems further inside than the breath. If you follow the instructions addressed to the imagination you will arrive at the most economical and physically subtle use of your voice.
 Read these steps before doing them.

■ *First allow the tiny quiver to happen like an electric current on center, then give in, let go, so that almost all the breath leaves your body (do not, however, push or squeeze it out as in the vacuum). At this point it might seem that there is nothing left to make a sound with. Without taking a new breath, think of relaxing even deeper into the interior and drop to a sound "huh" that is further inside than the breath.*

■ *Do the sequence: Quiver / release / drop to sound further inside than the breath; / relax, and allow breath to drop back in to refill the center.*

Repeat the sequence.

■ *Pinpoint with your attention the place deep inside your body where the sound is found. It may seem to be right up against the spine behind the solar plexus. Register it as a definite physical place and label it the* inner center.

Repeat the sequence thus: Quiver / let go / yield deeper inside and find a sound on the inner center "huh" / relax the diaphragm letting breath replace. / Now touch sound again on the inner center without using the new breath that just replaced.

It should seem as though, when you touch sound on the inner center, no breath is needed to form that sound. It will only be when you relax after the sound is over that some breath will replace, showing that some breath was used.

■ *Try it again. Quiver / give / give in further to sound — release for breath to replace — don't use that breath. Talk again from the inner center "huh-huh" / release and realize that some breath was used though you did not use it. / Talk again from the inner center. / Relax and breath goes in.*

The conditioning being done here is to translate physical effort into mental energy. In order to communicate larger content freely, all you need to do is stay connected to the inner center and deliver more voltage from the mind.

STEP 2
■ *Find the inner center connection on "huh," then change the sound to "hey." Repeat "hey-hey-hey."*
Let the breath drop back in and decide not to use that breath but to let the "hey" 's happen again on the inner center. After each set of "hey" 's, let go inside and breath will replace. Familiarize yourself with the mental process that says "I am not going to use any breath for the sound but I will let breath replace after the sound."

Here you begin to deal directly with mind/voice unity leaving out the middleman breath.

■ *Go through the preparatory inner center sequence. Then, starting sound on "hey," continue, building up power and volume in the sound depending solely on mental, not muscular, intensification. Release for breath to replace. The increase in the intensity of the sound should come from inner strength leaving the outer muscles almost completely relaxed.*

■ *Try this contrast exercise to clarify the difference between external and internal strength. Shout "HEY" pulling your stomach muscles in as hard as possible. Make the big, outside, abdominal muscles do a strong movement inward punching out a loud "HEY."*

■ *Now leave the outside abdominal wall loose and send the same strong shout impulse to the inner center on "HEY."*

■ *Go from outer muscle strength to inner mental strength several times to experience the changing process and the different results.*

STEP 3
■ *Do a full workout of all the voice exercises from the point of view of the inner center, changing intensities in power and volume.*

STEP 4
Exploring
sensitivity and
power through the
imagination
■ *Stand about twelve feet away from a wall and imagine that the wall is a huge canvas (at least 20 feet wide) on which you are about to paint a picture—a seascape. Read the instructions first.*

Paint a horizon line of bright blue waves right across the canvas.
Paint a large, simple ship. Red.
Paint a mast and two big white sails on the ship.
Paint a round, yellow sun.
Paint the rays of the sun.

Paint different sizes of white, fluffy clouds.
Paint little seagulls flying around the ship.
Sign your name right across the bottom.

The paint is your breath "ffff." Each new image creates a new breath impulse. There are large images that need large breaths (the horizon, the ship); there are medium-size images that need medium-size breaths (the sails, the sun, perhaps some of the clouds); there are small images that need short breaths (the seagulls, each ray of sun, the dots on the i's and the crosses on the t's of your name.) All impulses connect with the breath on the inner center and travel out through the torso on "fffff."

■ *Final instructions before starting: Be seized with sudden inspiration and the need to get the picture on the canvas quickly. Go.*

There are two things to note before trying it again or making your own landscape, portrait or still life. First, note that your breathing apparatus is being put through all the phases you exercised in terms of the six-sided box and the inner center. If you respond with strong inspiration to the largeness of the canvas and the blueness of the waves, you will use almost all the breath in the torso to draw the horizon line. As soon as you reach the end of the horizon line allow a quick impulse to take you to the ship image and breath will fly in to serve that impulse almost as it does when you vacuum the lungs. One breath per image. As you go fast from cloud to cloud and seagull to seagull, the impulses should activate the muscles much as they do in the medium panting; if you care to add a pointilliste effect for the spray off the waves, you can provoke fast panting-painting. The inner center is the electric socket into which the image impulse plugs.

Secondly, note that this is the basic pattern of breath/thought impulses in speaking. At least it should be if the mind/voice connection is sure. Every change of thought has a change of breath. Short thoughts have short breaths, medium thoughts have medium breaths, and long thoughts have long breaths. If the thought and the breath change together the voice inevitably starts on a new pitch with each thought and thus there is natural variety when the voice is free and connected to changing thought inflections. This central connection is essential to full communication. A change of thought that just affects the head is too shallow; only when the breath is involved deep in the body is the thought organic, and, only then is an actor involved profoundly enough to make communication worthwhile. It is always possible to tell (if by no other means) the depth to which an actor is involved in the text by the depth at which the breath is moving the body.

■ Try the picture painting again, and find out how you feel about each image. Don't think about *how you feel.* Let the image act directly on the center. There may not be much to go on, but there is a difference between the sun and a seagull which is worth a change of feeling.

The empty canvas acts upon the mind. The mind produces images which stimulate the breath and feeling energies. These energies release from the body to paint the canvas with the images.

This is the blueprint for a dialogue, simplified but accurate. Mr. A acts on the mind of Ms. B, either with his simple image, or with words and deeds. Ms. B's mind stimulates breath/feeling energies which find words in her mind to express those feelings which can then escape from her body to act on Mr. **A's** mind/body. A dialogue can begin. In a monologue it can be an external situation or an internal condition that provides the initial stimulus. Words are the added ingredient that complicate but do not invalidate the working process of the original blueprint.

■ Paint the seascape again, with exact imagery, and in your mind add a word description that lasts as long as each image and breath lasts. For example:

■ Thought: "A long horizon of blue sea waves."

"a long horizon of blue sea waves"

"a great red ship on the sea"

"two big, white sails"

"a mast . . ."

This is only interesting if you keep looking for and playing with your *feeling* response to the images and allow the words to be influenced by that. If you care nothing for the sea, ships and seagulls, then make a picture that you do care about. If you feel depressed by the pictures, then let your depression come out on the breath and affect the words in your mind. If you feel silly, then let the silliness come out on the breath and affect the words in your mind. It doesn't much matter what you feel as long as you let it out. Remember this: If you have gotten this far and you have read this, then it is impossible for you to feel nothing.

STEP 5 When you create your own picture you can make an image first and then add words as in the last exercise. Feelings respond more quickly to an image than to a word. When you read something from a page you start from words. Here is a very simple way to connect those words to breathing/feeling processes.

> Jack and Jill went up the hill
> To fetch a pail of water
> Jack fell down
> And broke his crown
> And Jill came tumbling after.

■ *Make a short, clear movie out of this with your breath, beaming the following five frames onto a movie screen in front of you on "ffff."*

A little boy and a little girl walking up a hill. ∅
They fill a pail with water from a well. ∅
The little boy trips as they start back down the hill. ∅
He falls down the hill and hurts his head. ∅
The little girl falls too and somersaults down the hill. ∅

■ *Allow the breath to be affected by the pictures, not by the words that inspired the pictures.*

■ *Run the movie again and allow the words to come into your mind, each line lasting as long as each frame and breath. Do not let the words dominate, let them pick up the feeling of the images and be influenced by them. Your feelings should be influenced by the images not by the words.*

■ *Run the movie again. Keep dealing with the pictures and the feelings and gently let the escaping breath/feeling be molded by your mouth into whispered words that last as long as each picture lasts. Let the words serve the pictures and the feelings.*

• Run the movie once more and this time let the feelings and images connect with sound which is molded in your mouth into spoken words that serve the images and the feelings.

This text is not very demanding in terms of emotional content but I hope you have found that if you are faithful to the image and feed it into the center, however trivial it may be, it does arouse some response on a feeling level which makes the speaking of the text more interesting.

Apply this process to more essential, more demanding and more rewarding texts: for example, any descriptive poetry, Japanese haikus, the choruses from Henry V.

According to different texts you will not only employ your mind's eye but your mind's ear and other mental senses as well. Let your screen be all round you, and let your mental impressions play on you in the same way as before. They drop from the mind into the inner center; from there they spread their influence through the nerve endings to become feelings. The feelings stimulate breath which escapes from the body carrying the feelings which are reformed into words as they pass out through the mouth to create on the external screen the scene you have internally seen, heard and felt.

Having suggested the Henry V choruses to work on, I would like at this point to bury an old ghost who says that it is necessary in performing Shakespeare to be able to speak twelve lines on one breath. This is not so. Sometimes it may be necessary to have the emotional stamina to maintain an unbroken line of emotional drive for twelve, sixteen or thirty lines, but within those there are a myriad changing thoughts, and breath must serve them by changing also. In an emotionally driving, demanding speech the breathing musculature must be very fit in order to supply fast, subtle changes to keep the thought content alive and to intensify as the emotions intensify, but the overall line is maintained intellectually. Emotionally it means nothing to be able to say in one breath: "In peace there's nothing so becomes a man as modest stillness and humility but when the blast of war blows in our ears then imitate the action of the tiger stiffen the sinews conjure up the blood disguise fair nature with hard favored rage then lend the eye a terrible aspect let it pry through the portage of the head like the brass cannon let the brow o'erwhelm it as fearfully as doth the galled rock o'erwhelm and jutty his confounded base swilled with the wild and wasteful ocean." It is not an impossible physical feat but the results belong to a style popular forty years ago and are meaningless to modern ears. I mention it only because young actors still occasionally ask for help in scaling this thespian peak under the influence of the eminent ghost.

The experience of an inner center for sound may help to bring the voice into more satisfying contact with the feeling. It is an experience you can benefit from at the outset of work on any character, any scene, to tap the deepest and truest parts of yourself, from which you draw to build. As you continue you will probably find that there are ex-centering aspects of feeling or character that take you away from the precise contact you have with your center, and that you become "centered" lower down or higher up in the torso. You move and speak from the genitals or from the brain as a particular character settles its peculiarities into one part of your anatomy or another. The pattern of tensions, inhibitions and habits that you have so painstakingly dislodged give space to the patterns that characterize the person you must portray. Or, it may be that at one point in a scene you feel a rush of energy from the soles of your feet flooding your whole body with warmth as you enter the action, and by the end you are fixed cold behind your eyes with everything dead from the neck down. The centers have utterly changed, and they will constantly change as your awareness picks up changing concentrations of energy. Thus, pragmatically, it must be stated that the center is moveable. As a purist, however, I would argue that there is an immutable center, one primary center of energy from which all movement and sound springs. All other apparent centers are places where that energy concentrates in the course of its journey through the body or is short-circuited by secondary impulse commands.

16: Articulation

The word articulation means "jointed-ness"; articulated is "jointed," "having joints." Such a definition is the least ambiguous way to describe the process by which vibrations flowing out through the mouth are cut up into words and become speech. It is an over-simplified account of the complex activity which transforms thoughts into speech, but the simple definition is the safest here as we move into the realm of words, and deal with the individuality of those who employ them. Since it is from their uniqueness that rich and creative contribution comes, the widest possible limits should be allowed as to *how* that contribution is made, in order not to curtail *what* is contributed. Speech is "the act of speaking; the natural exercise of the vocal organs; the utterance of words or sentences; oral expression of thought or feeling" (Oxford English Dictionary). Rules of speech do not have any place in the free development of such a natural ability. As long as there is a sensitive connection between the mind and the organs of speech, the natural ability develops as the mind develops. The exercises in this chapter will deal with speech only from that point of view. The muscles with which articulation is effected must be freed from limiting conditioning, and made responsive and agile enough to reflect the agility of the mind. No standards of "correct" speech will be given. Such standards last longer between the covers of a book than on the tongues of living people and are a lost cause because live communication will not sit still and behave. Much of what, in the past, was hopefully labeled Standard American, Transatlantic Speech or Standard English, was a reflection of class consciousness and as an attempted aesthetic rule of thumb is doomed to failure. Yesterday's beauty becomes today's camp and today's ugliness may pass for tomorrow's ultimate truth.

Lest the alternative to standards seem to be anarchy, I would emphasize that communication through speech involves not only a speaker but a hearer. If, therefore, what is said is incomprehensible, however much it may satisfy the speaker to say it, it fails as communication. Anything that distorts the message must yield in the interest of total comprehension, be it a personal rhythm that quarrels with the rhythm of the text; a vocal mannerism that leads attention away from the content of what is being said; an accent of such an extreme nature that the listener is always one beat behind, translating; or a lushly beautiful voice whose music is all that can be heard.

The one attribute necessary for dealing with such distortions is sensitivity. Any piece of good writing has its own palpable rhythm, texture, style. A sensitive interpreter will allow that rhythm to alter personal rhythms, will absorb the different texture to color the voice differently, will let the style shape and transform delivery. A sensitive performer, whether interpreting a text or not, will want a voice that serves the desire to communicate. Those who are relaxed enough to be able to hear what is going on around them and who respect an audience of one or many, will find that the most extreme regional accent will adapt to a point where communication is effected without sacrificing individuality.

Many accents owe their definitive regionality to a configuration of mouth muscles which trap the voice in one particular place. The nasality of the Midwest or New York develops a habitual posture in the back of the tongue and soft palate. A Southern drawl can give all responsibility to the jaw and leave the tongue lying dormant. The South Kensington drawingroom accent exploits a tiny portion of the tongue and the lips and an over-developed upper register, to communicate as little as possible from below the neck.

All these are habits of mind and muscle developed under the limited conditioning of one environment. Without condemning the initial conditioning, rigid extremes will inevitably be modified as new interior and exterior environments are explored; once the whole potential of a voice with three octaves, endless harmonics and unlimited textural quality is freed, changing styles are available to changing content. Limits lie only in the possible limitations of talent, imagination or life experience.

This chapter on articulation will offer suggestions for the most economical use of the articulating musculature. In this economy lies the potential for a sensitive connection with thought impulse.

With agile lips and tongue, free from the constrictions of habit, the one criterion for clear speaking is clear thinking.

The articulating surfaces

The front of the tongue, the middle of the tongue, the back of the tongue, and the surfaces above that they most naturally touch, are the most frequently used articulating agents. The two lips in varying contact with each other, and occasional contact between the top teeth and the bottom lip provide all other articulation. For all words to be formed in such a small space it will be appreciated that the articulating muscles must perform with the energy, precision and delicate teamwork of an acrobatic troupe. As with the breathing and laryngeal musculature, the coordination of muscle movements that mold vowel shapes while chopping them with consonants is too subtle and complex for conscious manipulation to do a better job than unconscious control. Once more, in the interest of an individual reflection of the mind, we must do no more than free the muscles from tension, limber them up and leave them to be played on by thought impulse.

This is most simply done by working with consonants which stimulate the separate articulating agents and make them supple enough to respond to the finer demands of vowels.

Consonants

STEP 1 ■ *Using a mirror to make sure that the message you are sending arrives in the intended muscles, focus your attention on the whole of your top lip and move it up and down, in the manner of a sneer that lifts the top lip up, exposing the top teeth and then stops, dropping the lip.*

Leave the bottom lip relaxed and isolate the top lip activity.

Repeat several times. (The muscles that move the lip in the sneer movement run from the nostrils through the moustache area.)

■ *Let the top lip relax and turn your attention to your bottom lip. Keep your teeth together so that your jaw is out of commission and pull your bottom lip down to expose your bottom teeth. Then relax the muscles to allow the lip to spring up. (The activating muscles run down into the chin.) Differentiate between movement of the jaw and movement in the chin musculature. The jaw bone must remain immobile during this exercise and all the lip and tongue exercises that follow.*

- Blow out through your lips to relax them.

- Repeat several times:
Top lip: lift, drop; lift, drop; lift, drop.
Bottom lip: pull down, release; pull down, release.
Blow out through both lips.

STEP 2   - Stretch your lips sideways, into as wide a grin as you can.
Then push them forward into as pursed a pout as you can.
Stretch sideways, push forward, keeping your teeth together and
your lips apart.
Repeat several times and then blow out through your lips to relax
them.

- Put your fingers into the corners of your mouth and pull them to
the sides.
Let them go like a stretched elastic band lets go.
Blow out through the lips.

- Repeat Steps 1 and 2 several times.

These are limbering exercises for the general musculature of the top
and bottom lips; more specific sets of muscles are actually employed
in forming consonants. Developing the independence of these
muscles from the jaw is of prime importance. When the teeth are
together the jaw is immobilized and the articulators must take over.

Repeat Steps 1 and 2 alternating teeth together and teeth apart to
develop the independent response of the lip muscles. When the
teeth are apart know that the jaw remains quite relaxed and still
while the lips move.

Step 3 should be prepared for with some of the humming exercises
(Chapter 6) and the sinus exercises (Chapter 10). Humming and head
rolling help free the vibrations, and mask resonance focuses them
forward to the lips.

It is important that the concentration on articulation does not cut
you off from center. There is a tendency, when working on the lips
and tongue, to lose the free flow of breath and vibration so that the
sound virtually starts where your attention is, in the mouth. Articulation should involve an increase of awareness that can encompass the
source of sound at the same time as the agents that handle the sound,
otherwise there is nothing to "articulate," just a series of isolated
"joints." This is not an uncommon disease in actors whose diction
is flawless but who remain unintelligible despite the fact that every
word is crystal clear. The overdeveloped muscles of the lips and the
tongue have destroyed the balance between voice and articulation
that is essential to full communication.

■ *Sigh out a hum and move your lips around on the hum, tasting the vibrations. Now play with the vibrations. Catch them and release them to explore a sense of the lips handling the vibrations and passing them on to the outside.*

mmmmmmm-uh mm-uh m-uh mmmmmm-uhmm-uh-mmmm-uh-m-uh
muhmuhmuhmuhmuh

Getting faster — bounce the vibrations off your lips.

■ *Now change the shape of the stream of vibrations as they leave your lips:*

mmm-ee mmm-eee

Make sure the "ee" comes out through your mouth. "M" is a nasal consonant and there will be a tendency for accompanying vowels to go into the nose too. This tendency can be counteracted by a sure picture of the forward flow of vibrations through the mouth, and a check to see that the tongue is relaxed.

■ *Change the shape again:*

mm-ey mm-ey mm-ey
mm-ee mm-ee mm-ee
mm-ey mm-ey mm-ey

■ *Change the shape of the escaping vibrations again:*

mm-aa mm-aa mm-aa
mm-ee mm-ee mm-ee
mm-ey mm-ey mm-ey
mm-aa mm-aa mm-aa

Observe that the lips do not have to change their behavior as the vowel changes. They can still go up and down, gathering vibrations and passing them on. The "ee," "ey" and "aa" shapes are made automatically as you think them (the back of the tongue moves subtly from a relatively high position toward the soft palate for the "ee," down to a flat relaxed position for the "aa"). For the time being, let the vowels look after themselves and focus your attention on the sensory experience of consonants.

■ *Practice the slow sensual connection between relaxed lips and the vibrations:*

mmmmeeee mmmmeeee mmmmeeeee
mmmmmme-e-ey mmmmmmme-e-ey mmmmme-e-ey
mmmmmmmaaaaaaa mmmmaaaaaa mmmmaaaaaaa

Explore the relationship of the lip surfaces to the vibrations. Don't think about "consonants." Don't listen. It should be the wet part of the lips that make contact and the muscles involved are minimal, stimulated by the vibrations. Make no unnecessary effort that could tighten the lips and kill vibrations.

- Now, changing the energy quality, go faster:

    mee-mee-mee mey-mey-mey maa-maa-maa

and then feed in changing rhythms. ("mēe" indicates weak; "mée" indicates strong.)

    mēe mēe mée   mēy mēy méy   mãa mãa máa

    mée mēe mee   méy mēy mey   mãa mãa mãa (repeat 3 times)

    mée mēe mee mēe mée
    méy mēy mey mēy méy
    máa mãa maa mãa máa (repeat 3 times)

    mēe mēe mée mēe mēe mēe mée
    mēy mēy méy mēy mēy mēy méy
    mãa mãa máa mãa mãa mãa máa (repeat 3 times)

    and so on.

Play with whatever rhythmic patterns you choose as long as you can make a pattern which you can repeat clearly and accurately. Every other part of the body must be quite still and relaxed so that the lips learn to be responsible and independent and the route from the brain to the lips becomes clearly defined.

Step 4 will take you through a similar pattern of exercises on "B." The same area of the lips is involved as for "M" but with a different quality of relationship to the vibrations. Find the exact point of impact between vibration and lip surface for the "B" sound which provokes a small explosive action.

STEP 4   ■ *Let your lips touch each other. Don't anticipate the sound. Be aware of relaxed lips (teeth just apart behind them, tongue quite loose inside the mouth, jaw relaxed). Now think the sound "B." What muscles begin to respond? Don't say the sound yet.*

If you do this slowly enough you may notice some unnecessary preliminary responses in parts of the mouth other than the lips. For instance, it is not uncommon for the base of the tongue to tighten as a sort of springboard for the "B," which results in an almost imperceptible glottal grunt just before the consonant occurs. This is not a very economical or crystalline rendition. Practice thinking the "B" directly onto the lips.

Think the
sound b.   ■ *Now lightly whisper the "B."*

The breath should explode forward off the lips in a tiny puff of air that is not trapped anywhere in the throat.

Feel and listen for the arrival point of the breath. If it is at all labored or hoarse then there is too much tension in the channel for the sound to be free when it occurs.

The quality of the breath when you whisper is the truest guide to the freedom of the sound that will happen when you add voice. Any tension will spoil the transparency of the breath which should sound as though it is flowing through the spaces of the throat and mouth, not touching the walls at all. The breath must be released from center and arrive on the lips without having touched anything else on the way.

■ *Allow the vibrations to travel the path that the breath has just traveled and voice the "B." Feel the tiny ball of vibrations explode forward off the lips.*

Play with that ball:

> buh-buh-buh

■ *Change the shape of the ball to something flat and thin:*

> bee-bee-bee

Change the shape again:

> bey-bey-bey

Change it again:

> baa-baa-baa

Leave the lips loose to respond to your thought. Don't make them work harder.

Play with the explosions of vibrations thus:

> bee-bee-bee bey-bey-bey baa-baa-baa

Then build the capability of lip response by applying the pattern of exercises followed for "M," increasing pace and changing rhythms.

Step 5 will leave the lips for a little and move to the front of the tongue. I differentiate between the tip of the tongue and the front of the tongue in order to emphasize that the most effective and natural parts of the articulating apparatus with which to produce "D," "T," "S" and "Z," are the surface of the tongue just back from the tip, and the upper gum ridge, which is the hard bony rim between front top teeth and the dome of the roof of the mouth. When the tongue, in repose, swells to fill the mouth cavity, its edges touch the teeth all the way round, and its surface touches the hard palate from front to back. The part of the front of the tongue that naturally meets the front upper gum ridge is the part to exercise for forward tongue consonants.

In order to isolate that area and strengthen it, here are some exercises making exaggerated use of the tongue's muscles outside the mouth so that when it relaxes back into the mouth it can perform with great ease in contrast.

STEP 5   ■ *Let the tongue slide loosely forward until the tip lies on the lower lip. Use a mirror to check that it is broad, thick and can lie there without any movement. If it is narrow and pointed, thin and flat or moves, it is not relaxed.*

■ *Lift the front of the tongue up to touch the top lip and then bend it down to touch the lower lip as though there were a hinge about 1/2 inch back from the tip that gives precise mobility. Move it up and down, specifically touching top and bottom lip.*

■ *Move the tongue from side to side, outside the mouth, touching the corners of the mouth. Make sure the jaw doesn't swing with it.*

■ *Alternate the last two bulleted sections several times.*

■ *Stretch the tongue, tip behind the bottom teeth as in Chapter 7.*

■ *Relax the front of the tongue once more on the lower lip. Then lift it as before to touch the top lip and this time find vibrations between the lip and the tongue to make the sound "L" as the tongue drops.*

It is as though you were speaking with your tongue outside your mouth, saying "luh luh luh" with the front of the tongue and the top lip. Let the tongue touch the lower lip again after each "L" sound.

■ *Repeat this tongue to lip movement going through the sequence of vowel shapes used for "M" and "B," all outside the mouth against the top lip.*

    lee-lee-lee   ley-ley-ley   laa-laa-laa

■ *Let the tongue slip inside the mouth and quickly and easily repeat the sequence, this time with the tongue patting the upper gum ridge for the "L"'s:*

    lee-lee-lee   ley-ley-ley   laa-laa-laa

■ *Alternate the last two bulleted sections outside the mouth slowly, inside the mouth fast.*

It should seem that the "L"'s inside the mouth happen out of the relaxation you experience after the exaggerated stretch of the work outside the mouth.

■ Build the capability for quick, lively tongue response as you did with the lips on "B" and "M," gradually increasing the pace and adding the changing rhythms.

■ Use the instructions for the previous five bulleted sections to explore the quality of action needed to produce "D":

dee-dee-dee   dey-dey-dey   daa-daa-daa

The "D" strengthens the tongue and makes it flexible even more so than the "L," because of the stronger impact between the articulating surfaces needed to explode the vibrations for this strong consonant.

Note the similar quality of handling that the vibrations receive for "B" and "D." For a true result it is essential that you really feel the vibrations between the surfaces. It is all too easy to have agile lips or tongue producing what is in effect a heavy "P" or "T" while the vibrations of sound remain fettered way back in the throat.

Follow the same instructions to explore the sound "nnn."

This is, obviously, in the same family as "mmm," a nasal consonant. The rim of the tongue is in contact with the upper gum ridge in the front of the mouth blocking the mouth exit so that the sound comes out through the nose. As soon as the front of the tongue goes down, the vowels following the consonant can and must escape through the mouth.

Play with the "mee mee mee" sequence and the "nee nee nee" sequence.

STEP 6   For the exercise of the third main articulating area, you must isolate an awareness of the back of the tongue making contact with the back of the hard palate just in front of the uvula. To prepare for this repeat some of the soft palate exercises learned in Chapter 7.

■ Then yawn and in the middle of the yawn bring the back of the tongue up to touch the soft palate interrupting the yawn to say "ng" as in the end of "sing."

Take the back of the tongue away from the soft palate continuing the sound which should automatically turn into "aaaaa."

Using a yawn stretch without actually yawning, repeat the back of tongue movement up and down with sound to make:

ngng - aaaa - ngng - aaa etc.
(the "g" is silent, the "aaa" is a yawn stretch)

■ Relax the mouth. With the back of the tongue this time hitting sharply but lightly against the hard palate just in front of the soft palate, explode vibrations which have the same quality as "B" and "D." If you follow this instruction accurately and calmly you should arrive at the consonant "G" which belongs to the same explosive family as "B" and "D."

Follow the, by now, familiar pattern of exercises from:

> guh guh guh

through

> gee gee gee   gey gey gey   gaa gaa gaa

making sure that the tip of the tongue stays relaxed behind the bottom teeth.

Make sure the jaw stays out of it, relaxed and still.

STEP 7   Finally put together a sequence of exercises going from lips to front of tongue to middle of tongue and back, which should be used as regularly as brushing your teeth to keep the whole set of articulators agile.

■ From lips to front of tongue:

> Buh-Duh-Buh-Duh-Buh-Duh

From front of tongue to lips:

> Duh-Buh-Duh-Buh-Duh-Buh

slowly, then gradually gathering speed. Alternate starting with the lips and with the tongue.

From back of tongue to front of tongue:

> Guh-Duh-Guh-Duh-Guh-Duh

From front of tongue to back of tongue:

> Duh-Guh-Duh-Guh-Duh-Guh

slowly first, then gathering speed, beginning alternately with the back of the tongue and the front of the tongue.

From lips to front of tongue to back of tongue:

> Buh-Duh-Guh-Duh-Buh-Duh-Guh-Duh-Buh-Duh-Guh-Duh

From back of tongue to front of tongue to lips:

> Guh-Duh-Buh-Duh-Guh-Duh-Buh-Duh-Guh-Duh-Buh-Duh

working it out slowly first to feel it through, then gathering speed. Precision and clarity are the criteria here.

Sigh the vibrations freely out from center throughout these exercises so that there is a steady stream of sound for the mouth to handle. These consonants can easily become clipped and dead unless you pay great attention to the connection of the voice with the articulating surfaces. As you become familiar with the "BDGD"'s you may find them going into a railway train rhythm. Exploit that or any other rhythmic patterns that occur to enliven the exercise.

■ Play with the BDGD's and their variants on scales, arpeggios or songs, always being aware of a release of sound from center that is not inhibited by the consonants but is handled by them.

Explore your range from chest resonance to falsetto using BDBD's, DBDB's, GDGD's, DGDG's, BDGD's and GDBD's, all the way from bottom to top and back down, sighing out, without skipping any of the rungs of the resonating ladder.

Improvise conversations using only BD's, DB's, GD's, DG's, BDGD's and GDBD's:

Questions and answers

Political arguments

Love scenes

Shopping expeditions, and so on all expressed solely through these sounds.

While doing these improvisations occasionally check with your partner or with a mirror to see whether the eyebrows are being unnecessarily active. Leave them relaxed.

It may be found that energy intended for the articulating muscles is picked up and rerouted through the eyebrows, the hands, the shoulders or a nodding head. All movements in these areas should be regarded as extraneous for the moment, and expression channeled exclusively into the center and the mouth. This does not mean that eventually head, hands and shoulders might not enhance communication, but in order to encourage responsibility in the lips and tongue, other areas should be left quite relaxed so that 100% stimulus can feed into the voice channel. As I've mentioned before, movement in the eyebrows is almost always a substitute for lively articulation or soft palate response; only a few specific feelings need the eyebrows for expression (a very incredulous question, considerable surprise, frowning). Excessive eyebrow raising always robs the voice. They go up instead of the pitch. They wiggle when lips and tongue should be racing.

STEP 8   ■ Follow the patterns described in Step 5 with a combination of the nasal consonants.

Múh-Nūh-Múh-Nūh-Múh-Nūh

Núh-Mūh-Núh-Mūh-Núh-Mūh

NGúh-Nuh-NGúh-Nuh-NGúh-Nuh (the G is silent)

Nuh-NGúh-Nuh-NGúh-Nuh-NGúh

Múh-Nūh-NGuh-Nuh-Múh-Nūh-NGúh-Nuh-Múh-Nūh-NGūh-Nuh

NGúh-Nūh-Mūh-Nuh-NGúh-Nūh-Muh-Nuh-NGúh-Nūh-Mūh-Nūh

Send all the "uh" sounds out through the mouth; only the consonants are nasal.

■ *Follow the same patterns and rhythms of exercises whispering "P," "T" and "K."*

These are the unvoiced equivalents of "B," "D" and "G," exploding breath this time instead of vibration.

No voice, whisper

> puh-tuh-puh-tuh-puh-tuh-puh-tuh
> tuh-puh-tuh-puh-tuh-puh-tuh-puh
> kuh-tuh-kuh-tuh-kuh-tuh-kuh-tuh
> tuh-kuh-tuh-kuh-tuh-kuh-tuh-kuh
> puh-tuh-kuh-tuh-puh-tuh-kuh-tuh-puh-tuh-kuh-tuh
> kuh-tuh-puh-tuh-kuh-tuh-puh-tuh-kuh-tuh-puh-tuh

With this exercise you can clearly check the freedom of the breath. It should not be heard in the throat, but should lightly and transparently flick off the articulating surfaces. Nor should there be any sense of holding the breath back in attempting transparency. Sigh out with complete abandon from center and insist that the lips and tongue catch and deal with the breath as it flies through the mouth. If there is no tension in the throat and a genuinely free contact between breath and articulators you may experience a sensation in the diaphragm of a fluttering panting. This is a useful guide to the purity of connection between the mouth and the center, and is created by the quick, repeated, minute stops on the breath applied by the lips and tongue as they form "P," "T" and "K."

Be very sure that the tongue comes down sharply enough from the hard palate to create a clean, sharp "T" and "K." If the tip goes too far forward onto the teeth you will hear a sibilant sound almost like a "TS" (the voiced equivalent would be "DZ"). The tongue, both at the front and the back, must drop far enough away from the palate to create a space through which the breath can escape freely, not scraping or hissing through a narrow crevice.

I will give only the briefest description of the other English consonants as they do not present much difficulty once the lips and tongue develop freedom and natural strength. I will explain where they are commonly formed for those who want to check their own effective usage. For those who have a specific problem, there are several other books which deal with the details of speech and speech defects which are outside the scope of this study.

Other voiced consonants and their unvoiced equivalents

LIPS:
"V" and "F"

"vvvv" is formed between the bottom lip and the top teeth as sound finds a way through that vibrates the lip against the teeth.

"ffff" is the whispered equivalent, with a softer relationship between lower lip and top teeth because breath provokes a gentler muscle response than vibrations.

TONGUE: "Z" and "S"	"zzzz" belongs to the same family as "vvvv" (categorized as *fricative*) and is formed between the front of the tongue and the upper gum ridge. To produce a really strong "zzzz" sound try sticking the front of the tongue to the gum ridge (leaving the tip of the tongue just lightly touching the lower teeth) and insist that the thought of "zzzz" pushes a path of vibration between the adhering surfaces. You will probably create "dzzz" to begin with, but use that to create the strong vibration and then cut out the "d."

"ssss" is the whispered (unvoiced) equivalent of "zzzz." If the tongue is relaxed there is no reason why a rich "S" sound should not naturally occur when it is thought. A sibilant "S" is usually the result of tongue tension that pushes the tongue forward and onto the top teeth where it funnels the breath through the cracks between the teeth creating a hiss, if not a whistle, that can be very distracting to both the listener and the speaker.

There is no one correct place for the "S" to be formed as there are so many variations in individual mouth structure. The best thing to do is to use the ear to discover where an "S" that pleases you occurs in your mouth. Start with the tongue relaxed and thick in the floor of the mouth, and then find the bit that most easily comes in contact with the rim of the gum ridge before it ascends into the dome of the roof of the mouth. If the tip of the tongue stays relaxed and you release a strong stream of breath out between the tongue surface and the upper gum ridge, a clear "sssss" should result. If not:

- Practice strong
  zzzzeee zzzzey zzzzaaa 's
with a long, clear, strong "Z" sound.

Then think "zzzz," but whisper the zzzzeee zzzzey zzzzaa's and listen for the result which should sound like a strong "sssss."

Now add vibration to the vowels "eee" "ey" "aa" while still thinking a whispered "zzzz" and you should arrive at a strong
  ssssee ssssey ssssaa
with an "S" sound that is different from your habitual one. It is up to you to find out where the difference lies in both your mind and your mouth and breath.

TONGUE: "TH" and "TH"	The sounds "TH" voiced (as in "the") and unvoiced (as in "both") belong to the same fricative family and are formed with the tip of the tongue trying to get out through a very small gap between the top and bottom teeth.

Maverick sounds made with the middle of the tongue almost rising as high as the dome in the roof of the mouth are "J" and its unvoiced equivalent "CH"; "ZJ" (as in "plea<u>s</u>ure") and its unvoiced equivalent "SH"; and "Y" which is a hybrid, half vowel, half consonant ("i" + "uh" = "y").

"R" is another maverick that answers to many rules and deserves a whole treatise. Here I will only express my personal opinion on two controversial points of usage and say that the American "R" should be restrained from pulling the voice back into the throat and the British actory "rrrr" should be banned as a trilled ornamental device in "classical" speech except for comic effect.

"W" is another hybrid vowel/consonant and I will use it here to exercise the horizontal articulating muscles ("oo" + "uh" = "w").

The face muscles crisscross each other vertically, horizontally and diagonally and, like any other muscles in the body, they need to be kept limber if they are to respond sensitively to motor impulses. Expressions on people's faces that seem to define them occur as the face becomes imprinted with characteristic attitudes that develop some muscles and leave others dormant. In order to have total availability in the articulating muscles, the horizontal and diagonal face muscles must be awakened as well as the vertical ones explored in Step 1.

STEP 10 ■ *Prepare by repeating Step 2.*

■ *Push your lips forward into the pouting position. Picture vibration as a tiny ball you can hold in your pouting lips. Allow sound, and play with the feeling of vibration on your lips, squeezing it and releasing it a little and squeezing it again ("oo-uh" on a very small scale).*

■ *You are now going to use your lips as a sling shot to throw the sound forward and off your face.*
Pull your lips sharply and strongly sideways into the grin and let the vibrations be catapulted forward in a staccato "wey."

■ *Look in a mirror as you do this and observe the diagonal stretch from the cheekbones to the corners of the mouth that occurs when you push your lips forward. Think of the sideways movement of the lips as a release from that stretch with the quality of the strong elastic of a sling shot being stretched and let go. As you let go notice that the cheeks are pushed up under the eyes.*

With a strong movement, a strong sound should result. Do not feel you are shouting but that a strong, sharp sound is the natural outcome of the strong, sharp movement.

- Repeat "wey" several times on one breath

    forward oo sideways ey
    forward sideways forward sideways forward sideways
       oo   ey   oo   ey   oo   ey

keeping the vibrations in tangible contact with the lips.

You should find that the middle resonating area is being employed so that it is as though the lips were picking up mask resonance across the very front of the face.

Blow out through the lips to relax them.

- *Take the "wey wey wey" all the way up through your range from chest to top of the skull. Use a mirror to make sure you still only go forward and sideways with your lips; do not allow the jaw to become involved.*

- *Go up and down the range again on "wey," this time with your teeth lightly closed to ensure the non-involvement of the jaw.*
Repeat with the teeth apart.
Using exactly the same lip movements, change the sounds to:

    will you will you will you

This changes the emphasis on the two-way diagonal cheek muscles to an active pull sideways on "will" and a release forward on "you." The tongue also gets a little workout on this exercise as it ripples the sound from its front on "L" to its middle on "Y."

- *With the full grin and the full pout explore the whole range of your voice from bottom to top and down again on*

    willyouwillyouwillyouwillyouwillyou
    will you wait willyouwaitwillyouwaitwillyouwait
    will you wait for willie willyouwaitforwilliewillyouwait
    will you wait for willie and winnie (etc.)

gradually increasing the pace and developing agility. As you go faster, relax the stretches a little; let the corners of the mouth flicker in and out like lightning.

- *Use the ascending range to ask a long question and the descending range to answer it.*
Repeat this pattern of question and answer covering the whole range with:

will you wait
will you wait for willie
will you wait for willie and winnie
will you wait for willie and winnie williams

Each one is repeated as often as can be fitted into the range and at increasing speed.

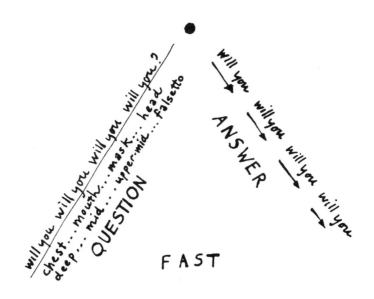

Step 11 gives you some idea of some speed games you can play to increase virtuosity and brilliance of articulation. The content is deliberately silly because these are drills, and serious material will only be belittled if used as exercise.

The key to greater speed is greater energy of mind.

STEP 11 ■ *On a five-finger exercise going up and down take the following phrase:*

Billy Button Bought a Bunch of Beautiful Bananas

Visualize Billy; picture the bananas; tell the story. As you go faster let the pictures speed up; the exercise's purpose is not to get mechanical as you go faster but to increase the mental agility without separating words from meanings.

Go higher on each repetition.

- *Get someone to fire the following questions at you at the end of each phrase and respond immediately:*

    "Was it Joe Button?"
    "Billy Smith was it?"
    "Billy stole the bananas?"
    "Did he only buy one banana?"
    "Were the bananas rotten?"
    "Did he buy apples?"

This may drive you mad but should stimulate the mind to deal with changing emphasis at speed.

- *Go through the same process with the following phrase to exercise the back of the tongue:*

    Gabby Gardeners Gather together and Gossip In Garrulous Groups
    *   doh   ray   mi   fah   sol fah mi ray   doh*

and add similar questions to it:

    "Were they reticent?"
    "Truck drivers were they?"
    "Was the gardener alone?"
    "Were they discussing their work?" and so on.

Silly but effective.

- *You should also use the ever practical Peter Piper.*

    Peter Piper picked a peck of pickled peppers
    A peck of pickled peppers Peter Piper picked
    If Peter Piper picked a peck of pickled peppers
    Where's the peck of pickled peppers Peter Piper picked?

Again find ways of awakening more and more mental energy to justify increased speed. Let skepticism grow to righteous anger at the unlikely story of Peter Piper ever having had the energy to pick a whole peck of pickled peppers in the first place. Or take on Mrs. Piper's anxiety at the non-return of her husband with the peppers required for dinner. Or spread hasty, gleeful gossip about a possible scandal.

In this way you keep the agility of articulation constantly in touch with mental agility and you will discover that as long as you can think quickly enough, you will be able to speak as fast as you like. You will, however, only be able to think quickly enough if you maintain real relaxation throughout your body while your mind, your breath, your lips and your tongue are stimulated. The more physical relaxation you sustain, the more mental focus you will be able to achieve.

Vowels

I will discuss vowels first in terms of fantasy. For years I have thought that a voice scientist told me (and indeed that I had seen, with a special kind of laryngoscope) that vowel shapes are initially formed on the vocal folds themselves. Although I am now firmly informed that this is not so I will persist in my discussion of vowels on the basis of what I consider to be a creative mistake. My aim is to engender respect for them, and a sensitivity of approach which will save them from distortion and colorless standardization.

There is intrinsic music in the basic physical nature of vowel sounds. It begins when the vocal folds assume approximations of the shape of the vowels conceived in the speech cortex, thereby changing the resonating pitch, whether on breath alone or with vibration. A simple demonstration will give a model of this process. Push your lips forward into a pout and blow breath through them. Listen for pitch. Now stretch your lips into a grin and blow breath through them. Listen for pitch. Be sure the tongue is completely relaxed so that breath goes directly onto the lips. You should hear a definite low sound when the lips are forward and a high pitch when they are pulled sideways. The vocal folds, in response to the thought "oh," form a round shape roughly similar to the lip pout, creating in miniature the shape for a low resonating pitch. In response to the thought "ee," the folds are pulled close together and air or vibrations going through the resultant narrow space create a higher pitch with that vowel. The main categories of vowels change the shape between the vocal folds, creating embryonic differences in their innate pitch. The subtleties of vowel differences need the soft palate, the pharyngeal walls, the tongue and the lips for refined modification and molding. On the vocal fold level, the shaping of vowels is deep-rooted in the involuntary nervous system. In the interest of preserving such subtle musicality the subsequent modifications must be highly sensitive. Any tension that clutches the breath will change the intrinsic pitch which depends for its existence on a free voice.

This correlation of pitch and vowel does not mean that "ee" cannot be said on a low note or "oh" on a high one. The introduction of a chosen pitch or the influence of a mood that dictates another pitch is what creates the harmonics of an interesting voice. Try the word "sleep." First as a lightweight, moderately high croon as though repeated to a baby. There is a place in the vocal range where there is a pure marriage between the "ee" and a middle-to-upper resonance. A single sound comes through. Now take the word "sleep" as though it were a hypnotic suggestion to be fed for its effectiveness through deep chest resonance. Listen for the low frequencies of the chest resonators harmonizing with another frequency which is that of the vowel. This is the natural richness and texture of speech. It is easiest to hear the harmonics with "ee" where the pitch and the vowel are unambiguous. The sharper listening needed for other vowels is good ear training. Try "moon." First slow, sleepy, low. Then quick, excited, pointing out the sliver of a new moon. The pitch of "oo" is low, harmonics coming in with an energy of speech that carries the voice high.

This is a dangerously analytical description of a process that can only work spontaneously. Thus, once more, the job is to render the muscles that pick up the motor impulses from the brain as free from tension, as subtle and as sensitive as possible and leave them to function involuntarily. The criterion for forming effective vowel sounds should be economy. Without economy there is no sensitivity, without sensitivity there is no subtlety, without subtlety there is little music. Therefore, if vowels can be recognizably arrived at without the use of the jaw, they should be. It is my experience that the jaw is unnecessary in the formation of vowel sounds, though its freedom of movement will add resonance to them. If you have to move a large jawbone around in order to achieve different sounds you are expending more energy than if you deal with the tiny muscles of the tongue and the lips.

The isolation of the lips and tongue from the jaw is important for clear speaking but take the principle to an extreme and you arrive at one of the most pernicious props of the elocution brigade: the bone-prop. This is a small instrument about an inch high that the student is asked to place between the teeth and bite in order to keep the mouth rather wide open and the jaw immobilized while the lips and tongue perform diction exercises. A cork is sometimes used, lengthwise, to provide an even greater obstacle to overcome. I have heard a speech from Shakespeare be subjected to the indignity of this test, and I am sure the actor who trains his diction thus on the text of a play will never effectively perform that play. The only way in which the lips and tongue can function in such conditions is with huge exaggeration and the diligent student will program gross mouthings in the place of articulation, killing any hope of natural music in speaking. Also programmed by this method is jaw tension which leads to throat tension and breathing tension.

The basis for work on vowels is primarily the freeing process that has been detailed for liberating, developing and sensitizing the whole voice. With a heightened physical awareness and some experience of the connection between yourself and your voice, it is safe to talk of ear training; in asking the mind to hear accurately and to choose and reproduce sounds by assimilation, not by imitation, you can develop a selection of sounds as rich as your own imagination can demand.

Any systemized work that I do on vowels is based on the vowel scale drawn up by W. D. Aiken and expounded in his book *The Voice*. It is good for British sounds but needs some adjusting to encompass American sounds. I find, however, that less and less specific vowel work is necessary as the voice becomes freer and freer. I also must confess that my approach to this subject is colored by a personal enjoyment of individual accents so I have not developed a series of vowel exercises that will ensure their demise.

Intermission: Workout

The following is a way of working through the whole sequence of voice exercises that incorporates everything taught so far. It emphasizes the stimulated breathing explored in Chapter 14, an altered order of exercises and a faster rhythm of work than before.

1. *General relaxation and physical awareness.*
2. *Rib cage stretching.*
3. *Vacuuming the lungs.*
4. *4 big sighs; 6 medium sighs; anticipation panting on center.*
5. *Natural breathing awareness.*

Spend about ten minutes solely on the breathing in 2 to 5.

6. *Touch of sound.*
7. *"huh-hummmmmuh"'s on ascending and descending pitches at twice the speed you usually go:*

Let the breath drop in fast with an awareness of the springy center created by the panting.

8. *Head rolling and humming. Fast in one direction, quick release inside for the breath, fast roll in the other direction. (Faster means freer neck muscles and several more rolls to one breath.)*

9. *Dropping down the spine on a hum. A quick drop down and up in one breath; release sound at the top. (Drop down giving in to gravity and bounce up from the bottom on the rebound.) Repeat several times.*

10. *Tongue exercises. Twice the speed and new rhythm.*

11. *Drop down, head downward and do the tongue exercises on ascending pitches.*

12. *Stay upside down and pant loosely.*

13. *Start upside down on tongue exercises then slowly build up spine on "hee-yuh-yuh-yuh"'s. Quick releases for breath in between.*

14. *Rest.*

15. *The whole panting sequence. Slow. Medium. Fast.*

16. *Soft palate. Fast in and out on whispered "kaa"'s at the speed of medium panting. The inner behavior of the diaphragm is the same during this soft palate exercise as during the 6 medium sighs of relief. Look for cooperation between the source and the channel.*

17. *Call across an imagined valley on "hi-i-i" with the inner energy generated by 16.*

18. *Drop your head back, free throat. Slow panting on whispered "haa"'s.*

Head up: medium panting on whispered "huh" 's; let the puffs of breath come straight from center to the roof of the mouth.

Head forward: fast panting on whispered "hee" 's; let the breath come sharply from center onto the teeth.

Reverse the order: forward, up, back, panting through the changing shapes.

19. Chest resonance

"haaaa-haaaa-haaaa"

Mouth resonance

"huh-huh-huh"

Teeth resonance

"hee-hee-hee"

Reverse the order and repeat several times, alternating with 18.

20. Call to free yourself on "he-e-e-ey." Shake it all out.

21. Sinus resonance. Do these alternately massaging with your fingertips and moving the sinus muscles up and down, and alternately hanging head downward and standing upright. Mid- to upper-register pitches.

22. Nasal resonance. Do the fast panting with pleasurable anticipation, then use that energy to ping the vibrations into the nose bone, quickly across the cheekbones and freely out of the mouth.

23. Do the whole sequence of panting.

24. Vacuum the lungs.

25. Use the energy generated in 23 and 24 to send the voice into your skull on falsetto "keee-eee."

26. Fast excited panting.

27. Fast falsettos going higher and higher with gathering excitement and instantaneous release from excitement for the ingoing breath.

28. Deep chest "hey" 's.

29. Range from bottom to top on "he-e-ey";

Range from top to bottom.

Range, loosening tongue on "huh-yuh-yuh-yuh" all the way from bottom to top and top to bottom;

Range, loosening jaw with hands throughout the sound;

Range, shaking whole body loose as sound travels from basement to attic to basement;

Range, dropping down and up the spine several times on one breath.

30. Articulation. Limber up the lips and tongue without sound. Corners of the lips forward and sideways on "wey's" "willyou's" "willyouwait's."

Range, on "wey wey wey . . ." from bottom to top and top to bottom.

> BuhDuhBuhDuhBuhDuh DuhBuhDuhBuhDuhBuh
> GuhDuhGuhDuhGuhDuh DuhGuhDuhGuhDuhGuh
> BuhDuhGuhDuhBuhDuhGuhDuhBuhDuhGuhDuh
> GuhDuhBuhDuhGuhDuhBuhDuhGuhDuhBuhDuh

Speak it—sing it on ascending and descending pitches—do it through the range from top to bottom and bottom to top—do it slowly then as fast as possible—improvise.

Whisper:

> puhtuhpuhtuhpuhtuh tuhpuhtuhpuhtuhpuh
> kuhtuhkuhtuhkuhtuh tuhkuhtuhkuhtuhkuh
> puhtuhkuhtuhpuhtuhkuhtuhpuhtuhkuhtuh
> kuhtuhpuhtuhkuhtuhpuhtuhkuhtuhpuhtuh

Add other articulation exercises.

31. Speak a poem; sing a song.

As you become familiar with the voice limbering process, you can explore it in conjunction with body limbering.

This sort of workout should leave you feeling very wide-awake, never tired. If you are tired it means you have been pushing and have ignored the intrinsic energy in reflex action. Never "breathe in," it is exhausting. Breath will "replace" naturally, and with the panting exercises you have been developing natural agility and restoring the speed of natural reflexes.

Part four:
The link to text and acting

17: Words

If, in dealing with words, we are to tackle eloquence as opposed to elocution, we must approach language with courage.

Elocution, to paraphrase the Oxford Dictionary, is the art of public speaking insofar as manner and style are concerned. Eloquence, on the other hand, appeals to reason and moves the feelings "with force, fluency and appropriateness."

Elocution flourished in the 19th Century, a period when the unacceptable realities of emotional and psychological turmoil were well hidden under the disguise of manners and social style. This disguise was reflected in the style of 19th-Century acting, not noted for its subtlety, and indulgent in word mastication. Audiences enjoyed the sound of actors "chewing up Shakespeare." In the subsequent three-quarters of a century, taste has swung in the opposite direction and landed us in an aridity which passes in today's theatre for honest, unadorned speaking. The fear of indulgence has virtually deprived us of a serviceable form through which to communicate.

Both aridity and mastication are unnecessary extremes. The answer is to move toward a revitalized eloquence appropriate to our needs and an enjoyment of language without wallowing in it.

Before suggesting how we might arrive at this, I shall explain the background for the approach to words found in this chapter.

In the art of speaking, I take "form" to be speech, and "content" to be intellect and emotion. The balance between the two is seldom struck, but the second half of this century promises more hope for a fusion of *what* is being said with *how* it is said than at any time since the Elizabethans or the Greeks. Our Pandora's box of the psyche is open; we can say what we like about ourselves. Our desires, our fantasies, hates, loves, perversions, infatuations and our sudden flashes of spiritual insight are available as theatrical content which, at the moment, leaves form gasping and straining in the rear. We don't have adequate words to express how we feel.

The problem for us is that words seem attached to ideas and detached from instinct. Feelings, attached to instinct and experienced physically, have to struggle for verbal expression because words seem to belong not in the body but in the head.

The mistake has been the banishment of words from the body. Human communication has become fragmented and weakened, even false. To change this we have to take the risk of indulging in the sensual experience that words can give us when returned to their rightful home in the body. Our risk is that the vibrations of sound will produce sensations of extreme pleasure; they may also provide a direct road to pure emotion. The potency of these vibrations is familiarly understood in their deflection toward religious ends, but in Western culture, ever since the Puritans, we have denied ourselves that particular power in human communication. For safety's sake we have persuaded ourselves that print, logic, intellectual ideas and the spoken word are one thing while our bodies and feelings are another.

For the Elizabethans, verbal power was an essential part of the whole person, and was taught under the heading of Rhetoric in every grammar school. They believed that perfect man embodied emotion, intellect and soul in harmony (and the word harmony implies sounds). Such belief is implicit in 16th and 17th Century education which, even at grammar school level, was sufficient training for the actors of that time. The Elizabethan schoolboy spent more time in reciting Latin authors than in reading them (approximately six hours of oral work to one of study), and such repetition was used to work toward the *highest standards of Rhetoric.*

The Art of Rhetoric (developed some four centuries B.C. mainly to argue legal cases) was designed to "excite the passions of the hearers" as distinct from the Art of Logic which appealed to reason. Aristotle's "Rhetoric" argues that the master of Logic should naturally be the master of Rhetoric but, then as now, this was seldom found to be the case. The practice of Rhetoric meant exact appreciation of language-structure, and expressive use of the voice and body in its service; the use of characterization where necessary; and the desire to communicate to the listener the precise intention of the author. The Greeks practiced this art and so did the Elizabethans.

Cicero declared, in A.D. 90, "No man can be a good orator unless he is a good man," and "the perfect orator is the perfect man." Such a high standard of morality is hard to maintain, which is perhaps why Rhetoric declined as an art shortly after its birth and again after its 16th-Century revival. Rhetorical *form* was quickly exploited without regard to moral content and the result can be seen in the debasement of the words used to describe formal speech with the passage of time. The Greek word for both oratory and acting was "hypokrisis"; their instructors were "sophists"; the word "rhetoric" itself now has the connotation of artificiality and ostentation if not downright lying. But for the Greeks and the Elizabethans such words were free of pejorative meaning and Rhetoric was an art.

The significance of all this for me is that without the connection between "morality" and rhetoric, trained speaking becomes false, and that the theatres of the Greeks and the Elizabethans were not only peaks in Western culture but an essential part of life with both a popular and an aristocratic appeal.

Although Cicero might not recognize the attempt, there is a more enlightened search today for an equivalent of "perfect man" than at any time during the last four centuries. If the "perfect orator" means one whose style uses both passion and intellect to illuminate his subject, and who aspires, through truth, to the transparent revelation of a fully developed human being, then there are actors today who would admit their dream of perfecting their oratorical ability. They have idealism. There is today psychological exploration, emotional exposure, spiritual aspiration and a hunger for the means to realize ideal communication.

Modern Western education has severely hindered the development of a means by which the inner life can be revealed through the spoken word, and the huge split between brain and body that has been educated into us needs much mending when someone today decides to become an actor. Today, learning can travel from the page to the eye, to the brain, down the arm, through the hand, back onto the page, never having been absorbed into the whole chemistry of a person made of flesh and blood, breath and feelings, sound and movement. It was only a few years ago that a student enrolled in a public-speaking course at a Midwestern university had passed his final examination by maintaining, in front of an audience, a three-minute silence with a black bag over his head. There was communication (he received newspaper coverage as "The Black Bag" and people seemed to know what he meant). He was an effective symbol of such a low point in the art of speaking that there is no place to go but up.

Language began instinctually, physically, primitively. The extended roar of pain, pleasure or rage, was articulated into more detailed communication by muscles in the body responding to the demand of an evolving intellect. That intellect, needing to convey increasingly precise information, deployed muscles in the mouth to distinguish positive from negative reactions and gradually to describe objects and facts and handle the minutiae of language. It is inconceivable that when the mouth first started to make words it did so in a manner divorced from its normal exercise of chewing, biting, kissing, sucking, licking, snarling, lip-smacking and lapping. All these were practical activities with sensual rewards and palpable side effects of pleasure for most of them, anger or fear for one or two. Words have a direct line through the nerve endings of the mouth to sensory and emotive storehouses in the body.

That direct line has been short-circuited, and the beginning work to release the built-in art of eloquence must be to re-establish the visceral connection of words to the body. An awareness of their sensory nature must come before that of their informational purpose. This is not to say that intelligence is to be ignored but that, in order to redress the balance between intelligence and emotion, emotion must be given precedence for a little while. For a large part of any day our voices are programmed to convey information, the dry facts and figures of making appointments, exchanging news, shopping. The "shopping list" part of the brain has appropriated the voice almost entirely to its use, while the emotional and imaginative parts have to struggle for their rights in it.

For the ensuing exercises it is necessary to acknowledge that, however sophisticated his brain has become, even 20th-Century man is part animal. The premise will be that in the relationship of intelligence to emotion, intelligence *shapes* the emotion, rather than emotion being shaped and released by the intelligence. In order to be able to transmit the subtle power of the "higher" emotions that respond to ideas (love for a person or a place; anger at injustice; joy at the announcement of peace in the world; sadness at betrayals, or in response to a poem, a painting or music with a tragic theme) you must have experienced the transmission of the raw, inexplicable power of the "lower" ones (lustful need sprung from driving, unsatisfied instincts of sex and hunger; the pleasure and occasional ecstasy of satisfying those needs; the crude pain of a physical wound and its similarity to the pain felt at the wounding absence of a mate both resulting in the phenomenon of tears; the phenomenon of laughter that does not come in response to a joke but as an outlet for instinct-rooted joy: running headlong, naked into the sea on a hot day; rolling downhill in the first snow of the winter).

Unless the "heightened" emotion has been distilled from primitive sources, it will result in art that is frail, precious, esoteric, lacking the common touch that taps those parts of us that are shared by everyone. With that touch to link it with humanity, theatre, the most human of all the arts, can lead us to an ever-expanding spectrum of consciousness.

Taking words back to physical and emotional sources is not difficult once a few examples have been given and the guidelines understood. The exploration in this chapter is experimental and arbitrary. It is intended to spark further experiments and fresh ideas and must not be seen as a doctrinal stance setting the teaching of speech on the next rigid, twenty-five-year-long road.

STEP 1 This will explore the different effects that different vowel sounds can have on your feelings and on your body.

■ *Prepare your body to be a receiving instrument to be played on by the sound. You can lie, sit or stand, but whichever position you start from, the preparation must be the process of deep relaxation that results in a state of unblocked physical awareness through which vibrations can flow. (To begin with, the supine position is the most tension-free and therefore the most receptive.)*

■ *Center your attention in the solar plexus/breathing area. From that center sigh out a long, easy*

AAAAAAAAAAAAAA

Picture the stream of sound flowing from the center of the torso, up through the chest and throat, out through the mouth, down the arms, out through the hands, down through the stomach, into the legs, out through the feet.

Imagine the wide stream of AAAAAA vibrations as energy that can move your body.

Imagine that the electrical impulse for sound activates your body and your voice simultaneously.

■ *On each sigh-out of AAAAAAAA explore the feelings that are aroused by the sound and free those feelings through the sound.*

■ *Now think the sound*

EEEEEEEEEEEEEE

and feed it from your head down to your center.

Sigh out EEEEEEEEEEEEEE.

Let it flow through your torso and your limbs.

Let it stimulate your body into movement.

Letting your body take in the intrinsic quality of EEEEE, find out what differences (if any) there are between the mood of "AAA" and the mood of "EEE," and whether your body and your feelings reflect those differences.

■ *Now go through the same processes with*

OOOOOOOOOO (as in "food")

- *Feed in to the center alternately*
  AAAAAAAAA
  EEEEEEEEE
  OOOOOOOOO
in changing sequences.
Try to be true to the form of each vowel sound.

- *If you have been experiencing these lying down, repeat the exercises standing, so that you let the sounds move your body through space.*

STEP 2   ■ *Take three vowel sounds whose quality is intrinsically sharper, shorter and more staccato than the first three.*

a	(as in "cat")
i	(as in "hit")
u	(as in "cut")

Taking each in turn, drop them into the center and bounce them out of you as though the diaphragm were a trampoline.
    Pant with each sound.
    Bounce them up and down your range.
    Find out how they make you feel.

Play these short, staccato vowels into your body to stimulate movement. (It may be that only a small part of the body is affected by the small sounds. The quality of movement will differ if the quality of "i" is different from the quality of "AAAAA.")

STEP 3   ■ *Drop contrasting vowel sounds into your body one after the other to spark contrasting physical and vocal responses. For example:*
    u   AAAAAAA   i   OOOOOOO   EEEEEEE   a   AAAAAA
(This is to develop vocal and physical flexibility of response.) Vary the rhythm, always observing the contrast between short and long vowels.

There exists a very fine line here between a free sound/movement response, and the imposition of *invention* on the sound. Invention and creativity with sound belong in another kind of exercise. In these, the object is to see whether your body and your voice are capable of receiving, and realizing fully, the innate character of a particular vowel sound. You are imposing if, in search of variety, you force "OOOO" to go high and staccato, and "i" to be deep and legato, when the one is comfortable in deep resonators and slow warm movements, and the other feels more at home higher up the range while moving your hands and feet. Your variety will be exercised in the wide variety of vowels.

I have used as examples only the most obviously contrasting sounds. As you explore the influence on sound and movement of subtly different vowels such as the "e" in "bed," "ey" in "hate," "oh" in "hope," "aw" in "walk," "o" in "hot," you will, if you persevere, develop the sensitivity of your muscles and your resonators to the point where they naturally reflect the delicate nuances of color and music that are the stuff of words.

STEP 4   ■ *Sitting, focus your attention into your mouth. (Capitalized consonants are voiced, lower case are whispered.)*

■ *Explore the physical sensation of*
   MMMMMMMMMMMMMM
between your lips.
Run it high and low, moving your lips.
Let the vibrations of "MMMM" feed from your lips down to your middle to find out how you feel as your mouth is used by M.

■ *Now explore*
   VVVVVVVVVVV
Let that consonant tell you its nature.
Then let your tongue taste
   NNNNNNNNNN
and ZZZZZZZZZZ
long and luxuriously, picturing a stream of vibrations forming an unbroken connection between the tongue and the upper gum ridge, and the solar plexus center.

■ *Play with*
   sssssssssss
   and fffffffffff
These involve breath and no vibrations of sound.
How do they make you feel?

■ *Play with*
   B   D   G
then with
   k   t   p*
Feel the staccato quality in contrast to the legato of the M's and S's.

■ *Play with contrasting staccato and legato consonants. (The vibrations of breath will explode from the staccato consonants in an unformed, neutral "uh" spoken with the voiced consonants, whispered with the unvoiced. The legato ones need no vowel sound.)*

Example:
   BUH ZZZ fff NNN kuh sss tuh DUH MMM

■ *Make a collection of consonants and develop rhythmic patterns for them. Example:*

    /   ·   /   /   ·   ·   /
   MMM kuh ZZZ fff tuh tuh DUH NNN
   (/ = long · = short)

Let a rehearsed rhythm pattern of consonants (such as the above) move your body.

STEP 5 ■ *Take two contrasting vowel/sound/feeling qualities and two contrasting consonant/sound/feeling qualities, for example, OO + a and ZZ + t, and mix them. Example:*
   OOOZZZta
   or ZZaOOOt
   or taZZZOOO

(Capital letters are long sounds; small letters are short sounds)
Elongate the long sounds, cut the short ones as small as possible.

Improvise with range, volume and rhythm changes on your vowel/consonant mixture.

Play them through your body so that they become an activating spoken music for you to move to. Don't sing; this is to expand the potential in your speaking voice.

Let your body feel the different qualities of the sounds and respond with flexible accuracy to them. Try not to use the sounds to express your energy, but let the sounds use you.

■ *On the basis of Step 5 explore the mix of three or more contrasting vowels and three or more contrasting consonants. Put them together clearly and develop clear rhythmic patterns so that you do not go into gibberish but exercise the ability of your body and your voice to respond flexibly to consciously thought impulses of sound which are as yet free from sense content. Example:*
   ZZZiFFFaOOOtapakEEEE
   and
   puMMMMMAAABOOOFFiSSSitaGOOGOONAA
and any combination you can put together that moves your mouth and your breath and your body to react with changing energies.

It is essential to the nature of these sound and movement explorations that the intrinsic character of the different vowels and consonants is not ironed out by the rhythm or subdued by other energies. You will find that as you allow these sounds to play through you, they stimulate energy by the simple impact of their vibrations. If your body is relaxed and your mind open, sound immediately generates energy. It offers at that moment, however, a channel through which you can express pent-up feelings; it is important to decide whether you are going to use the exercise as an opportunity for emotional release, or stick to the rules of this particular game. The rules are that the differing energies generated by the different sounds feed right back into those sounds and serve them.

Here are examples to illustrate this: If you were to start with

tipitaZZOOOOEEEE

it might arrive on a stave roughly thus:

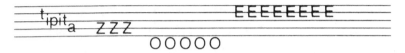

If you repeat it several times with rhythm and movement it might become:

pounded by the rhythm into one note. This must be avoided. Also try to avoid a release of arbitrary excitement that sends the sounds away from their resonance homes thus:

■ *To tune your awareness and your ear to the built-in music of vowels, whisper them. As you take away the resonance pitch of your voice you will hear clearly the pitch changes that occur as your breath passes through changing mouth shapes.*

STEP 6 Having played with sound and the articulation of sound within the form of the familiar vowels and consonants of our language, Step 6 will explore possibilities for articulation outside the limits of sounds in common usage.

■ *Preparation: Discover all the surfaces that can touch each other in and around your mouth.*

Your tongue touching the top and bottom lip, first the wet parts, then outside on the dry parts/touching inside the cheeks/inside and outside the teeth/the roof of the mouth/curling down, sideways and up to touch other bits of itself/the back of the tongue touching the back of the hard palate/touching the soft palate.

Your lips touching each other/wet bits touching dry bits curling in over the teeth/pouting forwards/lip touching teeth.

Teeth touching teeth, and so on.

■ Add sound to the above exploration.

Discover every possible combination of mouth surfaces to trap and release vibrations traveling out or in through the mouth to make sounds, and any combination of mouth surfaces to trap and release breath traveling in or out to make noises. ("Noises" are without the vibration of sound, such as sucking noises, teeth clacking, lip smacking and so forth. "Sounds" have vibrations.)

■ Sigh out a long, unformed stream of vibrations from center
    hu-u-u-u-uh
Picture the sound as material to be sculpted into shapes by your mouth.

STEP 7 The exercise: to choreograph a mobile sculpture of sound consisting of six or seven distinct shapes. Rehearse the movements your mouth goes through until you can repeat them accurately like a dance.

■ Use the combinations explored in the preparation to choreograph a word or sculpt one.

Here the idea is to create a "word" entirely through physical processes rather than through an aural/mental concept of a collection of syllables. The objective is to open up as many channels in the nervous system as possible which can respond to a word when it is received or conceived in the brain.

■ Rehearse the sequence of touchings and partings that your mouth goes through as it molds the vibrations, physically, in the way you might teach your feet a sequence of dance steps. (Your ear will hear the result, but you should ignore the aural feedback in favor of the physical awareness.) Example:
    1) hu-u-u-u-uh (stream of vibrations from center)
    2) back of tongue lifts to uvula, vibrations gargle between them
    3) front of tongue pushes down between lower teeth and lower lip then flicks out of mouth as breath sucks in, stopping the flow of vibrations
    4) front of tongue touches top lip finding vibrations between their surfaces

5) *tongue drops back into mouth leaving an open passageway for the vibrations*

6) *middle of tongue presses into roof of mouth stopping sound for a moment, then pulls away releasing the sound*

7) *teeth clack shut and open twice on sound*

You can use this "word" as the basis for a two-person improvisation. Find out how you feel as someone communicates a physically constructed word to you if you listen physically too. Take it in on your breath, breathing it down to your center, so that you are listening with your whole body. Then answer through your own physical word.

Allow these "dialogues" to continue for some time, maintaining the physical choreography of the word but allowing the changing energy of the dialogue to change its qualities (pace, rhythm, volume and pitch). Try not to let the word make *literal* sense. Do not domesticate the exchange by bringing it into a familiar context, such as improvising a scene in a supermarket, a boy-meets-girl scene, or an argument. The primitive, physical word should lead you into non-representational communication.

STEP 8   ■ *Using Steps 1 through 5 as models to suggest ways of anatomizing words, choose a word that is onomatopoeic and play it into your body, ignoring its sense as much as possible in the beginning. Examples:*

SPLASH RATATAT MURMURING SUSURRATION WHIP

If you were to take "splash" you might go through the following processes:

Feel "S," breath released from center, hissing between the front of tongue and the upper gum ridge.

Feel "P," the tiny puff of breath exploding from between the wet parts of the lips.

Feel "L," liquid vibration between tongue and gum ridge.

Feel "a," staccato, bouncing from the diaphragm, glancing off the roof of the mouth and out into the air.

Feel "Sh," the air softly foaming out between the middle of the tongue and the roof of the mouth.

Take them slowly, one by one, with a new breath for each.

Then gradually speed up the sequence until they join together in one breath with physical awareness dominating.

■ *Admit the sense and/or picture conjured up by the collection of sounds. Drop the word-sense into the center of your body and see what it makes you feel. Let the sense of the word and the vibrations of the word play on you: Explore the sound, the sense, associations, feelings, with movement.*

STEP 9 ■ *Take a word with a representational picture. Example:*

airplane	*butterfly*	*clouds*	*sky*	
earth	*stone*	*rock*	*brick*	
sea	*waves*	*stream*	*river*	*ocean*
fire	*flame*	*blaze*	*sparks*	

Close your eyes to see the picture clearly in your mind's eye.

Drop the image into your center.

Allow your feelings to respond to the image.

Let the feelings find sound that is molded by your mouth back into the word you started with.

Let the word serve the image. Let the feeling need the word to express itself.

STEP 10 ■ *Take a word with an abstract image. Example:*

love	*rage*	*giggle*	
purple	*red*	*blue*	*yellow*

Drop the word into center and see what happens. If you give yourself time, you may find that abstract images grow out of what the word means to you, or that the meaning makes direct contact with your feelings. Again let the feelings flow back out through the word that can contain and express it.

STEP 11 ■ *Play with small words such as*

for and to it if such now which what how

If you give each one time, it will make its independent character evident, with physical and grammatical propensities that can create their own abstract shapes in the mind's eye. Normally subdued by the more powerful images to which they are attached in a sentence, their separate qualities can add nuanced, vivid color to inflection.

STEP 12 ■ *String together a sequence of the words you used in Steps 8 through 11 in any order without making sense. Example:*

butterflies blue giggle murmuring

Exercise your ability to let one image (representational or abstract) follow another in sequence and to let feeling flow in response from image to image. You may hear or see the image in your head and beam the image down to your middle. Or you may directly see the image in the center. There is no rule about this, but let as much of your attention as possible stay with the feeling flow. If the images want to change, let them.

One after the other let each word/image/feeling find accurate reflection in your voice. Slowly first, to be sure of precise, moment to moment connection, then faster without letting one word rob another of its independent character. Don't, for instance, let "blue" color "butterflies" or "giggle" affect "murmuring."

Make some sense grammatically out of the words. Example:

The murmuring blue butterflies giggle.

Now, as you put "blue" and "butterflies" together they will form a new image from the two separate ones, but the composite picture is more powerful by virtue of the strength of the components. Add "murmuring" and the three make one whole, mobile picture; the "giggle" comes in and breaks the picture up, changing the feeling.

- Example 2:

no sense: blaze ocean ratatat rage yellow
grammatical sense: The ratatat ocean blazes into yellow rage.

"Ocean" is one picture. "Ratatat" added to "ocean" changes the picture. "Blaze" is one picture. "The ocean blazes" is a new picture. "Rage" might be red when it is alone but it has to yield to the "yellow rage" of the ocean.

The point of this exercise is to allow the individual words to influence your voice, giving a phrase or sentence more life to feed on than just the overall sense. The first example has, deliberately, little sense to it, but it does convey the information that those butterflies were giggling. The general feeling of the sense is giggly and that can be the one tone to emerge from the sentence, in which case the facts that they were murmuring first and were colored blue could be immaterial. In the second example the general impression is of anger, but there are descriptive specifics in the picture which can be communicated if the voice is sensitive to the influence of "ratatat," "yellow" and "ocean."

The dangers of this are so obvious that they hardly need comment. Memories of kindergarten poetry speaking ("the sun is in the sky" pointing heavenward, voice with upward inflection, "and the earth is down below" looking down, dropping the voice) may give one pause. But these exercises (not a method of speaking) are designed to start moving the voice from within, to make it come alive to a sensory and imagistic inner world. Once it is made flexible and sensitive in this way you can return to the job of communicating textual sense with a voice naturally susceptible to para-textual influences. The extremes of color and image will be smoothed into serving the sense inflection but sense need no longer be the sole inflectionary authority in speech.

18: Texts

This book is deliberately confined to work on the voice, without reference to a text. Ideally, voice work should feed organically into "acting," "speaking a text" or plain "speaking" without conscious application of technique. If the work to free the voice has been deeply absorbed, the person will be naturally freer; the person and the voice will be unified. In many instances the natural connection happens. Someone will go from a voice class to an acting class and experience a totally new freedom that has only partly to do with the voice. It might seem superfluous to mention the advantage of doing a warm-up before going on stage or into rehearsal, but there are actors who are still surprised at how well a rehearsal or performance went after having first done a voice workout. The aim is not just a well-tuned instrument but a continuously reopened road leading into and out of the creative center.

There are, however, ways by which the actor can build a conscious bridge from pure voice work to acting through specific work on a text. In this chapter I will only point out how the underlying principles governing the voice work found in this book may be applied to the exploration of a text. The process, initially simple, leads to delicate, fascinating complexities; thus, though I can offer general suggestions, the specifics of such an approach are beyond the capacity of this book.

Here are some general observations and suggestions relating to the voice and the text, starting with my feelings on how *not* to work.

Interpretation of the text must not be imposed from the outside, it must be released from within. When the blocks and limitations of conditioned thinking are removed, depths of understanding are uncovered beyond the scope of acquired knowledge. The task is to allow the text access to those depths and let it play on you.

Because a spoken text is revealed through an individual who is unique, it makes no sense for another individual (for instance, a teacher) to say how any given text should be spoken. It is vital, however, that every detail of what the text contains should be understood by the speaker. Unless the speaker has found out exactly *what* he or she is saying, *how* it is said will be arbitrary, narcissistic and misleading. (This may seem overstated, but it is my experience that half the actors playing Shakespeare understand less than 20% of what they are saying; the other 80% of their speaking is attitudinizing in sound.) It is only laziness on the part of a teacher or a director to take the short cut of telling an actor *how* to say a line rather than sharing the understanding of that line. Such teaching or direction demeans the actor's intelligence, saps confidence and diminishes individual creativity. I am against the use of any text that one day might be spoken by the actor on the stage as an exercise to develop vocal skill. It is dangerous to practice your ability to differentiate between long and short vowels, to sound final consonants, to produce upward inflections on most parts of a Shakespeare text, for example. One day you may find yourself playing a character who speaks those particular lines on which you labored with obedient ear and diligent lips and tongue. It is surprisingly hard to persuade the character to be anything but a diction expert at that moment, leaving an inexplicable hole in the internal logic of the scene.

I once worked with a very good actress who was playing Viola in *Twelfth Night*. She had spent a year at drama school studying the "score" of Viola's ring speech as an exercise in vocal flexibility, phonetic exactitude and the ability to reproduce the precise inflections for conveying the correct sense of the speech. She was completely blocked on that speech and, good as the rest of her Viola was, whenever she reached the ring speech the play went dead. She showed me the "score" she had studied. It was in a book devoted to scholarly analyses of meaning, and to mapping the exact vocal inflections for communicating that meaning. The score made complete sense of the speech and the author's argument was incontrovertible—on paper. But the part of the brain which receives such knowledge and can be trained to imitate and reproduce patterns of sound through eye and ear is far removed from the fertile, creative part upon which an actor depends. In the case of the Viola I worked with, patterns laid down in her speech cortex and labelled "correct" had made ruts that no new emotional or imaginative discoveries could eradicate.

In finding out what the text contains, in the case of verse or heightened prose an actor must learn about scansion, rhyme, rhythm, word-balances, puns, hyperbole, short and long vowels, voiced and unvoiced consonants, pace, volume and pitch, the meaning of forms and so on, but this should expand awareness and deepen understanding, not impose "the correct way to say the text." It is food for the intellect and develops the intellectual strength necessary to provide form for the content of emotion and imagination.

I am also against textbooks that print the text of a good poem and mark the places where breath should be taken. First, it is to me sacrilegious to use great poetry as a gymnasium where the student may flex the abdominal muscles, increase chest expansion, or practice the acrobatics of articulation. Second, if you are occupied with parceling out your breath until the next breath mark arrives and then making sure you are inhaling correctly, you leave little of your mind free to deal with the poem itself. Third, if your thought/feeling/breathing apparatus is unified and centered, you only need to understand the poem in depth for the breathing to follow the emotional line naturally and for thought-change and breath-change to be simultaneous and spontaneous. Breathing problems do not exist if the voice is free and the feeling true.

This relates to a tendency among teachers to use only the texts that are printed in a textbook as exercises. This means that certain poems are done literally to death. I feel that for their own sake students should be encouraged (persuaded — even forced) to read and choose texts for themselves from a particular author's works or within a particular style or period that serves the purpose of their phase of development.

Working with poetry helps the exploration of deep levels of perception, imagination and emotion. Poetry insists on the discovery of different rhythms within the body and the mind and thereby disarms the imagination. Words in a good poem are charged with a power that penetrates deep. In realizing the work of a great poet, you relinquish the singularity of personality and enter the atmosphere of universal experience. With poetry, what is being said cannot be discovered by the brain alone. Poetry is understood through the mind, the heart, the spirit and the viscera; ways of absorbing a text into all those areas must be available.

Here, now, are a few positive and practical ways of working on a text.

Text implies the word in print, and once in print the word impinges first on the external, visual sense. For the actor there has to be a conscious translation of the seen word into the heard and felt word. The word *seen* is inert; the word *heard*, moves. If there is a conscious transposition from external visualization of the word on paper to an internal realization of the word in the mind, it will immediately find embryonic sound in the mind's ear, pictures in the mind's eye and, given a little time, will attract associations, memories and feelings.

the Western voice: conditioned by print

There is no knowing how much our Western voices have been conditioned by print over the last few hundred years of relatively widespread literacy. It is not hard, however, to imagine that too much reliance on silent, printed communication deprives the voice of nourishment. The spoken word is oscillating, transitory and free to move on the waves of sound. Sound waves actively affect the body that generates them and varying parts of the body that receives them. The printed word is static, permanent, trapped in time and space by the letters of the alphabet. (Nowadays there is generally more respect for the word in print than for the spoken word, as though the permanence of print gives automatic validity compared to the temporary nature of speech. The reduced power of the spoken word is sadly typified by the remark "I'd much rather read Shakespeare than hear him." This only proves that we have lost the ability to embody Shakespeare's words and give them their true life in sound and action; they were certainly not intended to be read rather than heard.)

The practical task is to transform the text in print to the text in sound.

The restoration of the word to the body was explored in the last chapter. With a *text* we must tackle the accumulated *sense* that those words make through their various juxtapositions.

In the work thus far we have paid little attention to the role of the intellect in human communication, although intelligence has been in constant demand. The attitude toward speaking in this book illustrates the relationship between emotion, instinctive impulse, sensory response, physical and vocal action. This working picture is completed by an intellect which molds all that into shapes that have sense and meaning. It is a formidable task and the intellect has a powerful responsibility if it is not either to be drowned in emotion or to rise up in self-defense and stifle anarchic impulse. Instead, it must channel impulse, emotion, sensation and sound with a brain power that offers equal partnership rights in the speaking process. The first stage of work on a new text should be slow, meditative, sensory, unintellectual. Allow hardly any interest to occur as to the overall sense of any phrase, sentence or paragraph. Ideas of sense will, of course, emerge, and they should not be censored; it is just that they will be replaced by new realizations many times before a final choice need be made.

■ *To allow this first slow process you can follow this simple procedure: Go through the relaxation exercises described earlier. Then, lying on the floor with the text beside you, explore, phrase by phrase, sentence by sentence, sometimes word by word, the images and ideas that are contained in the text. The steps might be:*

1. *Look at the page and find a phrase (not necessarily the first).*
2. *Close your eyes.*
3. *Without speaking, allow the phrase to swim behind your eyes and then drop it down to your breathing center.*
4. *Let pictures attach themselves to the words.*
5. *Free associate.*
6. *Let feelings generate round the pictures and associations.*
7. *Sigh out what you feel.*
8. *Whisper the words with the feelings they have aroused.*
9. *Let the words and the feelings find your voice.*

Randomly explore a whole speech in this manner, not trying to make sense.

In this process words are given a solid physical home, become sensorily familiar and create their own harmonic reservoir of association, memory, music and rhythm. This reservoir serves to give life, character and independence to the words which make up the overall sense.

Gradually the sense of the text will be revealed, along with a much deeper meaning than can be arrived at by purely mental effort. Obviously if the "text" is part of a scene in a play, the final sense will depend on interplay with other characters.

At this point reexamine the text on the page and search for information that will help make choices between the various possibilities that have been discovered in the first process; study the form of the text for clues to greater clarity of sense; use all the resources of the intellect to bring order to the creative chaos of your inner life. As soon as you speak the thoughts and feelings that have accumulated internally out loud, you hear how the thought sounds and the temptation is to repeat how it sounded, instead of recreating what was thought. This is why rehearsing and playing a scene over and over makes it easy to be mechanical, to get in a rut. One way to break the pattern of mechanical inflection is to remove the sound of the voice while playing the scene or speech for long enough to become reliant once more on real thought and feeling.

■ The process to follow can be this (I will illustrate the process with a "speech," but it applies equally well for two or more people in a scene):

1. *Do the speech as fully as you normally would in performance.*

2. *Go through a relaxation process, standing.*

3. *Whisper the first few lines or a paragraph. The breath should be free and unforced, coming from the center of the body, not touching the throat. Undistracted by the sound of your voice, explore the sense inside your head..*

4. *Stop; relax again. Go back to the beginning and whisper the same passage again. Allow fresh thoughts and feelings to emerge. Be ready to jettison the old ways of speaking the speech that your ear retains. Feel you can act with increased freedom because you are not responsible for how you sound. The weight of your voice has been lifted off your thoughts.*

5. *Stop. Relax. Walk around; shake out your body. Whisper the same passage a third time. By now you should have completely forgotten how you sounded before and be involved in releasing the inner processes that motor the speech.*

6. *Immediately after you have whispered for the third time go back and speak the passage. Don't listen to your voice. Keep your attention anchored to the thinking, feeling processes you have liberated.*

7. *Work through the whole speech in small pieces in the same way.*

Do not whisper long passages; you will condition yourself too much to silence. You are trying to recondition a speaking process.

Just because you are whispering and there is no noise do not let this become passive; you are transferring energy, not removing it. You should feel all the time that you are functioning as an actor, not as though you are doing an exercise. Mental and emotional energy must be asked to compensate for the lack of vocal energy and then continue to generate when the voice is restored. Mechanical speaking indicates that vocal energy is compensating for a lack of thought and emotion; the whispering is to be used to reverse that situation. The ultimate controls for the voice are the impulses of thought and feeling; without those controls the voice takes over as sound only and becomes empty and meaningless.

I would like to offer now some general suggestions for working on Shakespeare's text. Most actors would like to play Shakespeare at some point in their lives because acting Shakespeare has special rewards for his particular challenge. I can only give here the briefest suggestions for dealing with Shakespeare's text, and some warnings. For background reading I suggest *The Elizabethan World Picture*, by E.M.W. Tillyard, John Russell Brown's *Free Shakespeare* and Bertram Joseph's *Acting Shakespeare* for sound, practical information.

The following suggestions are given because most of the difficulties actors have with Shakespeare arise from the fact that they *think* they know what they are saying but all too often their understanding is very rough. Unless the text is understood with minute precision, the acting will be generalized and hard to sustain.

Actors should realize that Shakespeare wrote in a language that is four hundred years younger than the one we speak today. They should not assume they will understand all the words, the grammar or the construction. They should work with a good dictionary at hand, Onions' *Glossary*, Partridge's *Shakespeare's Bawdy* and whatever *Variorum* is available. They should not trust scholars and editors *more* than their own actor's instinct, but should not utterly scorn their suggestions. They should compare editions and be their own final arbiter in editorial conflicts over specific words.

They must viscerally understand the reason for verse and the reason for prose, and discover how to let form give power to content. They should play with, work on, explore, speak, a sonnet a week. Shakespeare's language should become absorbed into their bodies. She who would one day play Cleopatra, he who would one day play Lear should attempt the roles first when they are eighteen, again at thirty, at forty-five and fifty-five and as often as possible in between.

Actors playing Shakespeare must be brave enough to let their reality expand to fill the largeness of his people and the heightened speech of the poetic plane of their existence, not try to make them familiar and "true" to 20th-Century reality. This sort of domestication plays so against the textual quality that the speaking becomes increasingly false the closer it gets to contemporary rhythms and a strange, obverse melodrama emerges.

Finally, American actors must not let themselves be persuaded that there is a different "accent" which they should adopt to play Shakespeare. "Standard English" or "Transatlantic English" or "The Queen's English" are no closer to Elizabethan English than is American English. In fact there are many American sounds which are closer to those used in Shakespeare's day than their English equivalents (in England). Scholars have reconstructed Elizabethan English as it was probably spoken, and the usefulness of their research for actors is largely in the challenge of its robustness and the physical vigor needed to speak it. I am against the currently popular notion that some "standardization" of speech is necessary for a given company of actors in a Shakespeare play. Such surface considerations are usually a cover-up for bad acting and impoverished direction. Inasmuch as the plays are universal and reflect life, they should reflect the diversity of life and there is no standardization of speech in life. Nor is it likely that the actors in Shakespeare's companies spoke alike, coming as they did from all parts of England. To counter the argument that it is distracting to hear a strong New York accent next to a Southern and a Midwestern one, I repeat that any accent will be modified by freeing the voice and add that the actor who allows Shakespeare's text to influence and shape him as any good actor must, will be fulfilling the rich variety of sounds that great poetry demands, and will naturally remove the limiting stamp of regionality.

Essentially "work on the text" means letting the words of the text happen to you; finding ways to let the text impregnate you so that sensory, emotional, imaginative, physical and vocal discoveries are the foundation on which the intellect can build. This, in turn, becomes the foundation on which the speech, the scene, the character and the play are built.

19: Observations and opinions on voice and acting

In general the problem about "voice and acting" is: How does an actor work on his or her voice with self-awareness and a conscious desire to improve its function, and at the same time act, or learn to act, with unself-conscious absorption in the character and situation of the play?

This raises the whole question of actor training, which, if answered, might eliminate the problem, and I shall tackle that question later in this chapter. First, I would like to discuss in a more personal and anecdotal manner some of the voice and acting problems I have encountered, in order to illustrate the complexities involved in a subject where every individual presents a new amalgam of causal tensions.

It should be clear by this time that, basically, the problems all stem from the separation of the voice from the person, and that their root causes can be found in psycho-physical conditioning by family, education and environment. The implications of the fact that (in ninety-nine cases out of a hundred) a baby's first breath is taken in response to fear, shock and pain, are almost too profound to contemplate. Some hope for enlightenment in this area lies perhaps in the publication of Frederick Leboyer's book *Birth without Violence*.

Dealing, however, with repair rather than revolution, the remedies that I use are based on the exercises and the principles detailed in this book. Ideally the result is the integration of person and voice.

A voice teacher essentially deals with five different areas of voice work: training, "band-aid," coaching, development of skills, and experimental work. By *training* I mean the pure, virtually segregated freeing and developing of the vocal instrument, unencumbered by external material such as words. This can be deeply satisfying work. It should take place with no clamoring for results, with no sense of haste. It should be undertaken with the knowledge that one year's work will bring understanding, the second will provide practice and assimilation, and the third will reveal results and changes that are so natural that the student forgets that anything was learned. In the fourth year the student can go back to the beginning and rediscover the work on a deeper, infinitely more subtle level.

Band-aid means nursing an abused voice back to health. This can be done calmly over some weeks with the patient shocked into submission by doctor's orders, or in an atmosphere of crisis, waiting in the wings to administer enough aid to allow the patient to go back on stage with just enough voice to tear it to shreds again.

Coaching has several implications. It can mean helping the actor achieve the director's vision when the director is unable to communicate with the actor (substitute director), or helping the actor achieve the director's vision when the actor's ability is limited (substitute actor). In certain circumstances coaching can be very exciting: if the materials are good; a good script working on a promising actor. The assumption is that there are blocks (physical and vocal) preventing the actor's creativity from being fertilized by the script, or that those blocks are preventing the free expression of what has been created. Tension is either forbidding entrance or denying exit. The "coaching" means removing the blocks to allow the text and the human being to begin and complete their chemical process.

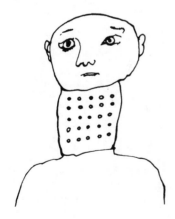

Band-aid: nursing an abused
voice

By *development of skills* I mean singing, dialect study and versatility in interpreting different styles of prose and poetry.

Experimental work is a broad category which includes the development of exercises for synthesizing sound and movement, exploring new territories of human sounds in collaboration with musicians, searching for the primitive links between instinct, emotion and sound in quest of the sources of language, and vocal improvisations on any number of given themes to serve any number of needs. This is where a voice teacher can exchange an ancillary role for one that is independently creative.

All the voice problems that I have had to deal with have included other problems in the body or the acting area. When a director says to me "can you do something with so-and-so — I can't hear a thing," he usually means "I can't *understand* a thing," "it is *unintelligible*." I worked on a production of *Henry VI* in which three young actors had to enter, one after the other, as Messengers 1, 2 and 3. Each was required by the director to speak quickly and with excitement, and in turn to raise the stage temperature by five degrees. The first problem was that each wanted to make his indelible mark on the play. The second was that the director did not have time to say more than "more excitement" or "remember there's a battle on" before going on to deal with the principals. Here are the three entrance speeches:

My honorable lords, health to you all!
Sad tidings bring I to you out of France,
Of loss, of slaughter and discomfiture:
Guienne, Champagne, Rheims, Orleans,
Paris, Guysors, Poitiers, are all quite lost.

Lords, view these letters full of bad mischance.
France is revolted from the English quite,
Except some petty towns of no import:
The Dauphin Charles is crowned king in Rheims;
The Bastard of Orleans with him is joined;
Reignier, Duke of Anjou, doth take his part;
The Duke of Alencon flieth to his side.

My gracious lords, to add to your laments,
Wherewith you now bedew King Henry's hearse,
I must inform you of a dismal fight
Betwixt the stout Lord Talbot and the French.

In trying to prove they could deliver the result the director wanted, the actors catapulted themselves on stage, rigid with tension, and blurted out a general pell-mell of incomprehensible words. The work that had to be done was to break down the speeches into specifically intelligible units, induce the actors to consider each messenger as a character with a life of his own, slowly put the speeches together again and, finding good reasons for haste, gradually build up the speed with which the thoughts could really happen behind the words. Then, if the lips and tongue still could not wrap themselves with sufficient agility around, for instance, "Guienne, Champagne, Rheims" we could do articulation exercises.

In the same production the actor playing Henry was young and had his first major role with this company. His sense of responsibility, coupled with a technically-oriented British drama school training which undermined any trust in his emotional strength, froze his upper lip and made his stomach muscles the rock on which he stood. The director was working closely with him so I avoided the acting side of the problem, trying only to loosen the frozen muscles of his neck, his face and his stomach. Finally, when the weather got warm, we would go out to a grassy hill by the theatre and he would roll down the slope, arms and legs flopping, body as loose as a fish, spouting speech after speech with clarity and emotion. In this case, the mental release achieved by violent physical release helped transform the whole process of communication.

Working with an actor playing Charmian in *Antony and Cleopatra*, the problem was again "inaudibility," this time with a different cause. She had had little experience with Shakespeare but had the warmth and emotional sensitivity that were perfect for the part. She could not bear to betray her sense of truth by projecting her voice, and she could not be heard. She had, first of all, to be told that her instinct *not* to project was right. Freed from that responsibility she then had to find how to share her emotions more generously than before. We worked in the theatre, taking the voice away, whispering the words as she played the scene. The aim was for her gradually to expand her circle of awareness peripherally while maintaining her central sense of truth. She had to know that in sharing her interior experience, first with the stalls, then the back of the theatre and then the balcony, she lost nothing, and indeed that the more she "gave away" the more she had. I, sitting in each of these places in turn, could hear everything she said on the whisper as long as the emotions were free, the thoughts clear and the breath flowed easily; it was only when she strained to "project" that she became unintelligible. Voicing the scene again, she could maintain her inner concentration and outer awareness and her voice carried naturally throughout the theatre.

The word "projection" is dangerous, suggesting that the actor throw the voice forward with an energy separate and different from the acting energy. Whenever a director says "Project!" or "Louder, I can't hear!" or "A little more diction, please!," energy is taken away from the emotional and mental content and transfers to the voice.

A common problem the voice teacher is asked to solve is that of

. . . the lost voice

"the lost voice." It is rare, however, for an actor to "lose" the voice utterly. It is usually possible to find a few remaining notes, sometimes in the upper register, sometimes in the middle, and sometimes low down. If the actor has the discipline to concentrate on maintaining what clarity there is, apparently sacrificing "acting" in the process, the voice will be exercised and will strengthen with correct use. Nearly always the restraint needed to do this will reveal to the actor where false acting choices had been made, leading to effort and strain.

Fear of losing the voice is one of the main causes of losing the voice. The vocal apparatus is very strong physiologically and very sensitive psychologically. There is, for instance, no physical reason for losing your voice if you have a cold, although psychologically you may think it impossible to utter a word. The hoarseness that comes from misusing the voice is often described as laryngitis, but true laryngitis is an infection of the larynx and the word should not be misused. I am much more inclined to help the actor who says "I've been straining, my throat hurts, I'm hoarse and I don't know what I'm doing wrong" than the one who says "I've got laryngitis" which begs for sympathy and imputes cause to some outside force.

There is a psychological battle to be fought against losing your voice if you have a sore throat, and the first thing to know is that it is relatively rare for the vocal folds themselves to be affected, so that physiologically there is nothing to prevent continued free production of sound. However, the pain and discomfort in the throat will irresistibly draw the mind's attention to it, and as your mind fixes in the throat you begin to speak from the throat. It is a difficult vicious circle to break. Added to this is the probability that energy is low and the muscles in the breathing apparatus will reflect this lack, so that vital support is diminished at the very time it is most needed to take pressure off the throat. To avoid losing your voice when you have a cold or sore throat you must double the attention you pay to your breathing. Insist that the mind detach itself from the throat and center in the diaphragm area to become an auxiliary engine for the weakened natural processes. Do consciously what usually happens automatically in your breathing. It is twice as important to do voice warm-ups if you have a cold. Never give in to that part of your mind that says "You'd better save your voice for the show"; "It'll do you more good to sleep for half an hour." Sleep *and* warm up. If you feel too blocked up in the sinuses to do the humming exercises, do twice as many humming exercises twice as gently. And do three times as many breathing exercises as usual.

If you ever go to a throat doctor's office you will find it crammed with actors and singers, the very people who should know how to look after their throats. Unfortunately it seems easier to take a muscle-relaxing pill than to go through the discipline of reconditioning usage. It is panic, conscious or hidden, that fills the doctors' waiting rooms, for nothing cuts off the voice's lifeline of breath more effectively than fear spreading through the fibre of the diaphragm and squeezing the muscles tight.

There are very few voices that cannot be repaired if damaged. Basically the rule is that if you strain your voice momentarily because you are reaching for something unfamiliar or are tired and start pushing for energy you don't have, always do a repair job then and there, or as soon after the event as possible. If you are hoarse *after* a performance, spend half an hour consciously relaxing and gently going through the humming exercises, tongue and resonance exercises. In the same way that a boxer or an athlete has a massage after the match to relax muscles so you should massage your voice back into good condition after heavy use. This kind of relaxation and restoration is of a totally different nature from that induced by a double scotch on the rocks after the show in the neighborhood bar.

One of the most demanding uses to which actors put their voices is singing. Ideally, the exercises in this book could be the groundwork for both the actor and the singer. Once the basic natural sound is free, it can be tuned, refined and molded to develop its propensity toward soprano, alto, tenor, bass or all-round ability. Often the singer's propensities are spotted early and developed prematurely with an inevitable drive to conform to the external standards of a teacher, before the person knows his or her own taste or trusts the inner need for expression as a valid motor for the instrument.

The actor who wants to sing should start with the thought that singing exists to carry emotional content that is too big for speech. Singing is intensified communication and greater release. The form, being more disciplined than speech, channels greater content with greater force through the outlet of specific, predetermined pitches. The actor is often intimidated by that form and studies singing as though it were a mysterious art which has little to do with the "ordinary" speaking voice. But unless singing is regarded as an expansion of self, letting it stimulate bigger feelings and a larger imagination, the result will be empty sound that could belong to anyone or even be made by a machine. The singer must stretch to take in increased demands on the attention such as pitch, rhythm and long phrasing. The stretched attention attracts more inner energy which awakens stronger vibrations of sound, and the whole person operates on a higher level to accommodate the process. It is, however, the same person as before. It is the same voice as the one used for speaking. The same breathing musculature, the same resonators, the same lips and tongue, all responding with greater strength to the greater demand.

There is considerable temptation to start using the voice as a manipulable musical instrument when you sing. You can get a clear, easy sound by focusing it into the nasal area, and you can consciously use the large outer muscles of the stomach to support it. You can consciously hold the rib cage up and out to preserve the breath for a long phrase; you can apply jaw movements to control pitch. But ideally the physiological instrument should be organically controlled by the psychological one. The clarity of the mask resonance should donate itself to the sound as it flows up and out through a tautly elastic soft palate, riding steadily on a breath that won't run out or collapse, because the mind is behind it. The way to sustain a breath through a long musical phrase is to extend the principle of "thinking through a sentence."

In speaking, the mind has to move moment to moment (word by word) through a sentence while at the same time driving the long line of a thought from beginning to end. The mind works on simultaneously vertical and horizontal lines. The vertical deals with words and the horizontal with overall sense. If, in singing, the horizontal demand is greater because of a long musical phrase, the mind has to work more powerfully. The vertical thinking in singing sustains pitches as well as words. With mind/body unity such increased mental potency must be reflected in greater physical power. The breathing musculature must be allowed to expand its potential naturally in response to gradually increasing demands upon it. The natural capacity of the rib cage will grow, and if there is organic expansion within a free, open, upright body, the lungs will not suddenly collapse in the middle of a phrase leaving its creator breathless with three bars stillborn for lack of oxygen.

The excitement of singing is so tremendous that it should be denied to no one. Anyone who has the desire to sing (and nearly everyone, secretly or openly, has that) owns the apparatus to fulfill the desire, but it is an extrovert pursuit and you can't be shy about it. Fear, in singing as in acting, is the number one enemy.

This kind of fear comes in strange disguises. Whereas, teaching in London I had become accustomed to confronting stiff upper lips, flippancy and unpunctuality as classic indications of inner panic, my New York studio provided me with a whole new gallery of the manifestations of fear. Some were more blatant than others. There was the man who catapulted through the door for his first class, arm outstretched to shake my hand, words of greeting tumbling out of his mouth as he shot past me clear across to the other side of the room where he bounced off the wall, turned, told me how tense he was, what his problems were, how he should deal with them, how he didn't deal with them, asked me to sit down while he told me something of his background, told me about his mother, his psychoanalyst, his acting teacher, his ambitions, how he couldn't breathe, how he hoped I could help him but feared I couldn't as his previous five speech teachers had failed, how he was sorry he had to leave early for another appointment – and careened out leaving me with my mouth hanging open, wordless.

On the other end of that scale of behavior was an actor who also happened to be an acting teacher. To his chagrin he found he was losing his voice in the classical play he was in and reluctantly came to me for help. But he could not bear the discovery that the cause of his problem might lie in his acting, and rather than face it, he would go to sleep. We would be in the middle of an exercise and his head would fall forward and a snore would escape. In the beginning he would only go off for a few seconds and he would not believe it when I told him he had slept. Then he started falling asleep in the middle of doing a speech, standing up. Finally, one day, after he had dropped off five minutes after he had arrived and I found I had no desire to wake him up, we agreed that perhaps he did not like working with me too much and we should part.

The person who really tested my self-confidence, however, was the actor who having survived one lesson, arrived for her second, rang the doorbell, took one look at me and said "Where's the bathroom, I have to throw up." For several sessions after that we would get to a point where she would have to retreat to the bathroom to evacuate her anxiety, but that point gradually arrived later in the hour and eventually she and I co-existed with mutual ease.

To avoid such fears, and prevent related problems, the actor should have a groundwork of good training in acting, body and voice. In this country such training has only recently begun to be available to young actors on an organized basis and it still leaves a lot to be desired. There are many unanswered questions about how training should be done and what kind of theatre it is designed for. It is a highly visible fact that today theatre comes in so many different shapes and forms that demand so many particular talents, that no

acting school or studio could possibly cater to all of them in a program that lasted less than ten years. Here are several general categories that come immediately to mind (there are others yet more specialized):

Straight plays (including American classics such as O'Neill, Odets,
Williams, Miller); musicals; Shakespeare and the classics (two or
three categories subsumed in one here); black theatre; improvisational
theatre; ensemble theatre groups where the actors create the play;
children's theatre; circus theatre; political theatre; visionary theatre
(where a way of life is involved and the private visions of the director
are served).

In each of these theatre forms an actor must use him or herself differently in order to be true to that form. There cannot be a standard
criterion of truth, good for all forms. For if a single standard is sought,
one loses the rich pleasure of diverse theatrical experiences, each
valid (when well done) in its own right. What is "true" acting for
Tennessee Williams creates falsehood in Shakespeare. The way the
mind and the body must work for Restoration theatre would be ab-
surd in a personal improvisation. The particular skills needed to act
in a musical are obvious. But those necessary for improvisational,
visionary or political theatre have to be developed and do not respond to the questions that a character in a "straight" play must ask
("Who am I?" "Where am I coming from?" "What is my objective?").
The essential excavation of the sub-text of modern plays is a different exercise from the approach necessary for a Shakespeare text. The
words of Shakespeare contain all the clues an actor needs for character, emotion, thought and action. The acting approach is one thing
if the important messages are expressed *between* words, *behind* lines,
despite the words spoken as so often in contemporary plays, genuinely reproducing the ambiguities of modern communication; the
approach is quite different if, as in most pre-Ibsen plays, and em-
phatically in Shakespeare, words and thoughts take place simultaneously. Ambiguities are there but they are expressed, not suggested. It is fatal in Shakespeare to think first and then speak, or to
think one thing and play another, unless the text specifically demands it. Pauses are built into the rhythm of the writing and are
clearly indicated by the verse structure. To add to those intended by
the playwright is an indulgent imposition of today's "truths" on
those of another age, whose character was as unlike ours as a village
in the heart of New Guinea is to Manhattan. The familiar rhythms of
contemporary thought and speech applied to Shakespeare have been
the cause of many a four-hour production of a three-hour play.

Other specialized acting demands are made in creative ensemble
work. Here the actors must be willing to contribute things that are
deep and personal from which a theatre piece can emerge, and neces-

sities for collective theatre work are physical dexterity and a sharing of a common level of being. The Open Theater was the archetype whose integrity and genius gave the first dignity to such creations.

Another example of specialized needs is the black theatre, which has demanded that the black actor exploit rhythms and inflections of speech and movement that give recognition to the vitality of "street" language. It draws on the rituals of brotherhood, the signs, the added music of sounds that can weave a world of meaning around words, turning their dry, dictionary sense inside out, stretching them to breaking point, throwing them out in favor of a gesture or a vocal punctuation mark. It has to be liberated from an educated bias against such a violation of English and it has to be "learned" by many black actors.

Actors must have tested their ability to create accurate representational theatre almost as a test of the ability to reproduce their own created selves. From this grows the security all actors rely on to change their natures, their rhythms, their points of view, to shift the balance between their minds and their emotions according to the varying natures, rhythms, opinions, life-values, of such a varied library of writers as Brecht, Chekhov, O'Neill, Bullins, Beckett, Leroi Jones, Sam Shepard, Ibsen, Congreve, Shaw, Shakespeare and so on. It takes a singer years to develop a repertoire that encompasses Mozart, Palestrina, Verdi, Mahler, Schubert, Fauré. Very few who are steeped in such composers will also tackle Berio or even Britten. A dancer trained for classical ballet who crosses the line to Martha Graham, Merce Cunningham or Alvin Ailey will seldom retain the ability or the desire to dance *Swan Lake*. Yet actors expect and are expected to be able to play a classical repertoire just because they are talented.

One cause of the lack of clarity on the subject of acting lies in the muddle that persists on the subject of actor-training. Although the parallels are not precise, it is interesting to note the contrast in the attitude to training in the other performing arts of dance, singing, music. In these arts there is a definable body of work devoted to training the instrument through which the art is transmitted: the dancer's body, the singer's voice, the musician's handling of the violin, piano, trombone. Years can be spent on developing and understanding the instrument and there are exercises designed for that purpose (barre exercises for the dancer; scales, arpeggios, technique exercises for the musician). Separate from those there are the works of art to be performed, and as these are studied, the artist and the instrument develop further.

The actor's instrument is composed of the body, the voice, the imagination, the emotions, the brain, and the life experience of the human being that actor is. Thus an actor's training should begin with training the *person* that he or she is before developing the *actor* he or she will become. In the old days a young would-be actor went to ballet classes to learn graceful control of the body, to singing classes to learn to manage the voice, and to an acting studio to study whatever approach to acting a particular teacher had devised. It would take a well-integrated personality to triumph over such fragmentation of function. It is now understood, in theory at least, that taking a human being apart, developing the parts and trying to put them together again to make an artist, is at best an unreliable business, and at worse dangerous. With the growth of psychological insight there is acceptance of the idea that training the body and the voice and the person should be a synthesized process. The genuine practice of this theory has yet to be seen. Having taught for some years both in an excellent English drama school and in the best attempt yet made at a truly professional American one, I would like to outline my ideal, purist and largely unrealistic basic training program for an actor.

Hypothetical four-year actor-training program

In the first year, students have an hour a day of voice work and an hour a day of movement work consistently and continuously throughout the year. This work is an un-doing process. It begins to break down physical and vocal habits; it teaches an initial ability to relax tensions consciously. This ability slowly increases, expanding physical awareness, allowing more and more subtle connections between the mind and the body and a corresponding heightened state of being. Precise rapport between the approaches to the body and the voice is essential. While a student is attempting a deep re-programming of the route from motor impulse to muscle, it is important not to create chaos in the nervous system. If the student obeys the movement teacher's instructions to tuck in the behind, turn out the toes and support the torso with strong, contracted stomach muscles, and then goes into the voice teacher's class where the stomach must hang out, the knees go loose and the spine assume full responsibility for remaining upright, there will be confusion in the motor cortex if not general short-circuiting in the morale. It is important, too, that the gradual shift from *releasing* the body and the voice to *developing* their strengths be synchronized.

A similar synchronization is found with the acting work. Following the principle of release then development, basic acting consists of individual and group exercises to open up the imagination, break down reserves between people, liberate the emotions. This is delicate, very personal work, hovering on the boundary of psychotherapy. It is vital that there be a framework and a vocabulary that constantly refers the results back into the demands that acting will make without shirking the personal implications. There are several good improvisational approaches that can do the job effectively, each depending on the talent and understanding of the teacher, who must be able to provide the security and apply the pressure to get to the hidden core of a person. The aim of this basic work should be to remove habitual controls, to recognize and learn to follow impulses, to trust vulnerability, to explore and become familiar with different emotional conditions, and to begin to know how to enter and inhabit the interior world of self. The first two or three months of a first year's acting can be spent on such personal work without recourse to a written text.

The second step in acting makes use of two-character scenes from contemporary plays, preferably characters reasonably close to the age and experience of the students. (The improvisation classes continue with the emphasis on evolving group sensitivity and stretching imaginative horizons.) To begin with, in the scene work, the focus is on the personal processes between two people. The text is there to serve the student, so that the accurate interpretation of the scene as the author intended is subordinated to the ability of the student to personalize and make the words deeply true for him or herself. The two people involved (not yet "actors") learn to listen, to hear with their feelings, to make available the raw material of their lives in order to vitalize the exchange between them, discovering how to make words and actions that are not their own the outcome of an inner life that demands expression.

Balance is maintained between the emotional demands of such scenes and the stage of development the student has reached in voice work; hysterical screaming before the voice has been freed can set progress back considerably.

During the second half of the year several scenes are worked, each chosen to tackle a new area of personal exploration. By the end of the first year the students have a clearer idea of who they are and how they function, but may well feel that much has been taken away from them, leaving them in a sort of limbo. They are encouraged not to take a summer acting job, to take a vacation if possible, or, if they must earn money, to work at any job that has nothing to do with the theatre. The first summer is a gestation period. If they act according to what they have learned thus far they might never work again; if they act well enough to do a good job they will inevitably be going back to old tricks and patterns, thus effectively wiping out several months of de-conditioning.

There are other classes that can usefully take place in the first year: simple circus techniques such as juggling and tumbling. Ideally there should be two kinds of movement class. The Alexander technique marries perfectly with voice work and should be combined with more active movement exercises designed within the same philosophy (action results from the release of energy from an inner center.) Maximum effect with minimum effort is the criterion. Halfway through the year the voice teacher should add a class that aims to link the "technical" exercises with a text. Such texts must be very simple. They can be contemporary verse, a story written by the student, Japanese haiku, early Chinese poetry. As in the acting work the aim is to achieve a simple, personal connection between the words and self. To be able to talk.

There is usually more time available in the first year than later on, which gives an opportunity for some general education in such fields as theatre history, music, history of costume, psychology, anthropology, Marxism, museum visits, local politics, sociology and field research into how other people actually live. The less academic such education can be, the better. There is eternal distress at how little young actors know about the theatre, how out of touch they are with current events, how uninterested they are in politics, how they never go to museums or concerts and that they don't read plays. I doubt that an acting school can remedy all these ills but time may.

In general the second year concentrates on development and consolidation. Voice and movement continue with at least an hour a day on pure release and strengthening, and additional longer sessions once or twice a week to explore the application of what is being achieved "technically" to creative and interpretative work. Content, something to be expressed through the voice and through the body, is introduced in vocal improvisation and movement improvisation on themes, or with stories. By the end of the year there will be combined sound and movement improvisation. In the acting area a step is taken from personalization toward fulfilling the needs of the scene. Two-person scenes are still the most useful for this, but now the student recognizes that the character in the play may react differently in a given situation from the natural reaction of the person playing it, and ways of rechanneling that person's raw psychological and emotional material in unfamiliar directions are examined. The practical application of whatever acting vocabulary that pins down the reality of a character's existence within the confines of a particular play is relentlessly rehearsed. How to give flesh and blood, psycho-emotional answers to questions such as "Who am I?," "Where am I going?," "Where am I coming from?," "What do I want?," "What's my objective?," "What's the scene objective?," "What's the plot objective?" How to depend on interaction with the other character. How to trust the life of one moment and then another. Each new scene chosen should stretch and mold personal reality to fill characters and situations further and further removed from the person playing it. Different emotions are explored, unfamiliar attitudes are examined. By *doing*.

Expansion into three- and four-person scenes is the next step, and in the second half of this year the more specialized aspects of character work are defined.

One of the reasons I say that this is an unrealistic scheme is that it is hard to convince people who want to be actors that there are good arguments for not "doing a play" at the beginning of training. While the process of acting is being taken to bits and relearned it makes no sense to attempt to act a whole play. At the end of the second year, however, one-act plays are worked on or one act of a full-length play. The energy for sustaining a whole play is built gradually. The single acts or one-act plays are rehearsed under the direction only of teachers who have been involved in class work, and shown only to those who understand that a certain stage of growth is being witnessed, not a production. During the second year there are opportunities for bringing the various disciplines together. Team-teaching sessions place emphasis on how physical and vocal freedom can help liberate the creativity of the actor. The move from classes into rehearsals is conscious and studied. Young actors have to be taught the difference between learning how to act, and rehearsing a play, and there is a process halfway between teaching and directing that must be applied to the initial involvement of student actors with the first play they work on for an audience. At *least* six weeks are devoted to these rehearsals so that the principles of acting that have thus far been absorbed are applied with integrity. Before every rehearsal there is a voice and movement warm-up.

By the third year students are much more demanding. Whereas in the first two the teachers make the demands (in terms of vulnerability, discipline, stretch, work), in the third the students are beginning to feel their individuality and have a sense of themselves as *actors*. They begin to feel for themselves what their creative ambitions might be and how much work their bodies and their voices need to fulfill those ambitions. So *they* make demands of their teachers to help them with specific needs. It might seem that by the third year it would be possible to cut back on the "technical" work and concentrate more on plays, but in fact it is now that a thirty-hour day becomes necessary to accommodate the expansion of needs in all areas.

In general, the third year allows the student to practice the craft he or she has been learning in as many different kinds of plays as possible. Three or four different periods in theatre are explored in the course of the year, and two full-length plays performed for invited audiences. The emphasis in these productions is on the actors and the play, with only essentials in terms of costumes, sets, lights and props. A number of different periods can be explored in scene and act work, along with methods of doing background research on authors as well as the history, art, politics and social customs of the times.

In the third year students also extend their basic training in voice and body skills. Singing classes begin now, speech classes (dialects to be lost or acquired, problematic diction etc.), dance (period, folk, jazz), fighting (fencing, wrestling and whatever is "in" in Oriental fighting arts), acrobatics. Poetry speaking, (which has moved from contemporary through 19th century to 18th and 17th century, from narrative to lyric, from ballad to epic,) now gives way to a concentrated Shakespeare text class. Here, I would like to quote a comment made by Bernard Shaw on the dangers of learning to speak verse:

"To young people studying for the stage I say, with all solemnity, . . . leave blank verse alone until you have experienced emotion deep enough to crave for poetic expression, at which point verse will seem an absolutely natural and real form of speech to you. Meanwhile if any pedant with an uncultivated heart and a theoretic ear proposes to teach you to recite, send instantly for the police."

In the fourth year as many plays as possible are done before audiences and, if possible, taken on tour; outside directors are brought in to do productions; skills are sharpened and experimental work is encouraged alongside traditional theatre practice.

I do not see how an actor-training course that understands the importance of organic learning can cover the basic necessities of craft in under four years. By the end of that time a person has a groundwork of understanding from which to move out into the theatre and gradually become an actor through the next five or ten years of experience of plays. The training I have outlined may seem conventional but it is based on the belief that actors must be able to fulfill the classic traditions of the theatre before branching out into innovative experiment.

The logistical problems of my ideal program are probably unsolvable. For one thing, it is essential that the same group of teachers see the same group of students through the first three years. This means that new students are taken into the school only every fourth year. Not an economically sound proposition. Each intake should be no more than twenty four. By the fourth year this number will probably dwindle by attrition to at most fifteen.

No tuition should be charged since the generally accepted notion that unless you pay for your education you don't have an incentive to learn, is not relevant to training in the arts. It is far less true in theatre that "working your way through school" increases the appetite for knowledge. An acting student who works as a waiter until one in the morning and arrives at a movement class at nine the same morning to learn deep relaxation, will quite rightly fall asleep. Financial insecurity makes it hard for someone to become emotionally courageous. The acting student needs weekends and evenings for rehearsals, for scene work and homework. And there should be some free time left to have fun, to begin to accumulate some of the life-experience on which talent feeds, and to go to the theatre.

Sound-and-movement

I would like to conclude this book by talking a little about the work I have done in the area of combined voice and movement work.

Voice and movement classes, warm-ups and improvisation classes are proliferating, but those that I have witnessed seem to have little understanding behind them. They are often performed through bodies and voices which are almost deformed by tension. The result is double falsity created by two false instruments. Too often the extremities of the body twist, jerk and sway, while the voice manipulates noises that are born in the throat and die just in front of the nose.

The separate instruments must be trained in their separate freedoms, and each must plug into the impulse center deep in the body. Only then can they respond to the imagination twice as powerfully through mutuality, instead of performing a discordant duet.

I have hopes of devising a really satisfactory combination voice and movement warm-up, but thus far I find that if you put them both together you short-change one or the other. Someone will complain that their nasal resonance or their right leg has been left out. The best solution is to have about forty minutes of physical work that warms up each part of the body, encouraging sounds to happen whenever the person wants to release on sound; then forty minutes of voice work, covering the precise details of the whole vocal instrument (this is also a physical process), and finally to devote twenty to thirty minutes to sound and movement improvisation.

Apart from warm-ups, I have spent many years in sound and movement explorations, which began while I was teaching at the London Academy of Music and Dramatic Art. I joined forces with Patricia Arnold, who taught movement, and we started by working on the technical problems of moving and speaking at the same time. We spent hours sending students careening across the floor crying "Sovereign of Egypt, hail!" They were asked to imagine that they had run all the way from Rome, to trumpet "Sovereign of Egypt!" at the door, to end up on their bellies kissing Cleopatra's foot, and to insert a long, drawn-out "Hail" somewhere between the door and the foot. We were surprised at how difficult it apparently was, and much linoleum was polished. From there we progressed into purer realms where we fitted voice exercises and movement exercises together. This was somewhat external and academic. Finally we stumbled on the juice we were seeking in two onomatopoeic lines from Tennyson:

Unnumbered and enormous polypi
Winnow with giant arms the slumbering green.

The Kraken

People began to give their bodies to the images and let the feel of the words be the motor for their movements, and one of the main points of combined voice and movement work emerged: In having two channels of expression simultaneously available, there was the opportunity for a much richer release of imaginative energy.

The first stages of such work should seem like self-indulgent play, on the principle that until you have given pleasure to yourself, it is hard to know what you are giving to others. Then, whatever "form" is desired should channel the flood of "content," making choices, molding it into a shape that is packed with the energies of sound and movement serving a defined purpose. If the work is done in order to enlarge the people doing it, a spectator should see and hear the same thing occurring in the body and the voice, for both should be operating with the same set of dynamics. If, on the other hand, the objective is to create a dialogue between sound and movement, to orchestrate or choreograph them, then the dynamics may be contrapuntal. The first process is the one that interests me most, as it promises expansion of the actor into an augmented state of energy that can provide for spectators the electric experience that draws them to a desire for their own expansion. This magnetic power is the reason, I believe, for theatre as an art form.

The need to find a synthesis of voice and movement is obvious in the case of the actor whose body is expressive but whose voice is strangled, or the one who can speak well but moves mechanically, but beyond such technical imperatives there lies an area where the creative impulse can play the body and the voice simultaneously making voice-music that choreographs the body instantaneously from inside. This potential, released, can make its own theatre.

In the relatively new manifestation of the actor not only as interpreter but also as the creator of original theatre pieces, there is a growing field of abstract theatre in which the mastery of any particular skill can be used to tap the artistic possibilities of that skill independent of a "play." Working, for instance, with Joseph Chaikin on the Open Theater's *The Serpent* made new demands on my imaginative ear. I began to hear the potential for communication that lies behind words in rhythms and particles of sound. With the Open Theater we worked for the connection of sound and movement with the same subterranean impulse source; it became clear that those are rich depths that also must be plumbed for a full response to dramatic poetry.

Coda

The directions that attract me now have been revealed through periods of experiment with groups of actors in which we were seeking to open up corridors of dormant consciousness through which the subliminal power of poetry could move, sparking intuitive responses and stimulating vibrations of sound and movement which communicate with other people on an infra-verbal wavelength. We launched out on exploratory voyages, letting the voice and the body be blown and buffeted in every direction by the changing winds of different word energies. We exercised the mind's eye in its ability to see images conjured up by words, and let the voice and body be canvases on which mental shapes and colors could be painted. We searched for the actor's equivalent of abstract and impressionistic art, using sound and movement as our medium. We permitted words to inhabit and run riot in us unlimited by their literal sense. We were looking for the harmonics of the sensory, associative, musical, physical and emotional components that make a word. We wanted to make available the deepest and widest extent of our humanity for Shakespeare's poetry to work on; and, in general, to restore some of the red blood that has gradually drained from our spoken language in the last four hundred years. Our ambitions always ran out of time, but there were flashes of experience that showed these were roads to be traveled again.

I am interested in the mystery of what kind of theatre would emerge if actors were really liberated from the patterns and inhibitory limitations of habit; and if writers for the theatre underwent the same training as such actors, developing the same creative vocabulary. (Shakespeare and Molière were two great playwrights who were actors in their own companies.) What would happen if actors, working from pure response rather than from the interpretation imposed by personality, could fully absorb and be transformed by a text; what could they reveal in classical work? And how would writers and actors re-invent a theatre that matters for us today if their full humanity were accessible, unrestricted by accumulated physical and vocal evasions?

Today's actors, if they are to compete for audiences with the technological powers of film, electronically souped-up music and television, must generate within themselves an electric presence that transcends technological excitement. The power is in there to be tapped, and the expansion of the theatre experience into something once more significant, depends on going in, in order to come out; on tackling cause before result; on drawing the arrow back as far as it will go before releasing its pent-up energy to the target.

Kristin Linklater was born in Scotland in 1936. She trained as an actress at the London Academy of Music and Dramatic Art and subsequently returned there to teach voice production as Iris Warren's assistant. In 1963 she came to the United States where her work was immediately recognized for its organic answer to the actor's vocal needs. With her New York studio as a base, she spent the next few years working during rehearsal periods with the Tyrone Guthrie Theater; the Festival Theatre, Stratford, Ontario; the Lincoln Center Repertory Company; the Negro Ensemble Company and the Open Theater. She ran a training program for voice teachers in 1965 funded by the Rockefeller Foundation and in 1966 became Master Teacher of Voice in the New York University Theatre Program. She has run workshops with the Free Southern Theater, the Royal Shakespeare Company, the Conservatoire Royal de Liège and the National Theatre for the Deaf. From 1974 to 1977 she conducted a full-time, three-year program called The Working Theater (foundation supported) to train teachers in an integrated approach to voice, movement and acting.

Ms. Linklater has trained many teachers, some of whom are presently teaching at the American Conservatory Theater; the Festival Theatre, Stratford, Ontario; the National Arts Centre, Ottawa; and in theatre training programs at New York University, Carnegie-Mellon, University of Wisconsin at Milwaukee, California Institute of the Arts, Neighborhood Playhouse, Circle in the Square, and many others. Currently **Ms. Linklater** is involved with Shakespeare & Company, a year-round training and performing classical theatre company based in Lenox, Massachusetts.